On
Education

'Clearheaded, acutely perceptive, and utterly lucid, this is the one book about education which everyone can and should make time to read.'

Randall Curren, University of Rochester, USA

Praise for the series

'. . . allows a space for distinguished thinkers to write about their passions.'
The Philosophers' Magazine

'. . . deserves high praise.'
Boyd Tonkin, The Independent (UK)

'This is clearly an important series. I look forward to receiving future volumes.'
Frank Kermode, author of Shakespeare's Language

'. . . both rigorous and accessible.'
Humanist News

'. . . the series looks superb.'
Quentin Skinner

'. . . an excellent and beautiful series.'
Ben Rogers, author of A.J. Ayer: A Life

'Routledge's Thinking in Action series is the theory junkie's answer to the eminently pocketable Penguin 60s series.'
Mute Magazine (UK)

'Routledge's new series, Thinking in Action, brings philosophers to our aid . . .'
The Evening Standard (UK)

'. . . a welcome series by Routledge.'
Bulletin of Science, Technology and Society

HARRY BRIGHOUSE

On Education

Routledge
Taylor & Francis Group

LONDON AND NEW YORK

10/17/11
ww
$21.95

First published 2006
by Routledge
2 Park Square, Milton Park, Abingdon, Oxon, OX14 4RN

Simultaneously published in the USA and Canada
by Routledge
711 Third Avenue, New York, NY 10017

Routledge is an imprint of the Taylor & Francis Group, an informa business

Typeset in Joanna MT by
RefineCatch Ltd, Bungay, Suffolk
Printed and bound in Great Britain by
TJ International Ltd, Padstow, Cornwall

British Library Cataloguing in Publication Data
A catalogue record for this book is available from the British Library

Library of Congress Cataloging in Publication Data
Brighouse, Harry.
    On education / Harry Brighouse.
        p. cm. — (Thinking in action)
    1. Citizenship—Study and teaching.   2. Education—Aims and
objectives.   I. Title.   II. Series.
LC1091.B69 2006
370.11′5—dc22   2005012978

ISBN10: 0-415-32789-X (hbk)
ISBN10: 0-415-32790-3 (pbk)

ISBN13: 978-0-415-32789-3 (hbk)
ISBN13: 978-0-415-32790-9 (pbk)

Acknowledgements

The ideas in the book have been evolving over the past six years or so, and I have been able to divide that time between the US and the UK. I enjoy a work environment so conducive to doing good work that this book really ought to be better than it is: I inhabit a Philosophy department which not only tolerates, but encourages and rewards my explorations into educational issues and am lucky to be connected to two terrific research centres on education – the University of Wisconsin, Madison's School of Education, and the University of London's Institute of Education. I wrote the final draft while holding a 2004 Carnegie Scholarship, for which I thank the Carnegie Corporation of New York.

My thinking has been subject to too many influences for me to list them all accurately, so I apologize in advance, but I must thank those that I can. I can trace debts to all the following people: Richard Aldrich, Dianne Gereluk, Elaine Unterhalter, Alison Kirton, Michael Apple, Geoff Whitty, Sally Power, David Halpin, David Carr, Doret DeRuyter, Terry McLaughlin, Janet Orchard, Kats Katayama, Lorella Terzi, Carrie Winstanley, Paul Severn, James Conroy, Shelley Burtt, Eamonn Callan, Stephen Macedo, Kenneth Strike, William Galston, Amy Gutmann, Brian Barry, Rob Reich, and Wally Feinberg. Randall Curren identified me as a philosopher of education before I was one, and has been a constant source of support and ideas since. Thanks are particularly due to Alison Kirton for permitting me to draw, in Chapter Seven, on ideas we first developed in a co-authored paper. Tony Bruce got nine readers to comment on a draft, all usefully. Tony's own guidance and patience throughout the project have been indispensable. Adam Swift suggested that I write the book, and provided extensive commentary on the penultimate draft, as well as other kinds of help less easily quantified. While I claim sole responsibility for all errors contained herein, of all people mentioned I must emphasize that Adam should not be blamed for any of those errors, only for prompting the book to be written. I'm especially grateful to Caroline Brown for reading a whole draft and providing immensely valuable feedback, and also for getting in touch so long after our own schooldays together. Daniel Hausman and Erik Olin Wright have consistently encouraged me to work on these issues. Thanks are also due to Jeremy Sutcliffe, my editor at the *Times Educational Supplement*, for giving me the opportunity to try out some of my ideas on a much larger audience than I am used to, and for helping me with 'translation'. I owe a special debt to Francis Schrag, whose own thinking and work have influenced me enormously. Most, if not all, of these ideas developed in daily conversations over many years with Lynn Glueck, whose experiences as a teacher prompted many of my thoughts, and tested the rest, and to whom I owe so much more.

Several chapters draw on and develop ideas I have published elsewhere. Several passages in Chapter One were previously published in 'Civic Education and Liberal Legitimacy', *Ethics*, vol. 108, no. 4, 1998, pp. 719–45 and I am grateful to the University of Chicago Press for permission to publish that material here. Other chapters develop ideas first published in

'Faith Schools in the UK: an Unenthusiastic Defence of a Slightly Reformed Status Quo', in Roy Gardner (ed.), *Faith Schools: Consensus or Conflict?* (London: RoutledgeFalmer, 2005), 'Should We Teach Patriotic History?' in Kevin McDonough and Walter Feinberg (eds), *Cosmopolitan Values and Collective Identities*, (Oxford: Oxford University Press, 2003), and (with Alison Kirton) 'Compulsory Citizenship Education in England: Problems and Prospects', *Delta*, vol. 53, nos 1&2 (2001).

Most academics are academics because they did well at school. Extended reflection on my own schooling and that of others has made me quite aware of how much I owe to the countless hours of socially undervalued and under-remunerated work that talented and dedicated teachers put into my education. I can't thank them individually, but in the preface to this book more than any others I'd like to take the opportunity to thank them collectively. Bedgrove Middle School 1970–75, Burnham Grammar School 1975–79, Peers Upper School 1979–81. Thank you.

Introduction

Schools are increasingly expected to make up for the failures of other social institutions. For the first time in history, we expect schools to educate everyone, not only those whose parents were educated themselves. We expect them to do this despite keeping high proportions of children in poverty, and despite surrounding children, at ever younger ages, with a fervently anti-intellectual popular culture. We expect them to deal with the emotional consequences of fractured – and ever more complex – family arrangements. Our economy demands long working hours from adults, and even when both of a child's parents live together, they frequently need to work those long hours in order to feel they are keeping up with their reference group – and in order to provide their children with the material goods they expect from watching television and observing their peers. Schools therefore deal with significant numbers of children who do not have a single adult whose life they share when they leave the school gates. Our economies are also complex and wealthy; we expect schools to train a labour force that is large and diversely tooled. At the same time schools must deal with the demands and interference of parents who feel, reasonably enough, a sense of entitlement to have a say over what happens to their children in the 15,000 hours or so they spend in school. Politicians, parents, employers, and even children, are constantly proclaiming on what schools should be doing.

This book joins in. In Part One of the book I elaborate and argue for a set of principles that schools, policymakers, and educators should adopt. These principles centre on the interests of children, rather than those of the wider society, business corporations, churches, or, for that matter, parents. In Chapter One I argue that children have a right to learn about a range of ways of living and to the kind of education that will enable them to reflect on their own way of life in the light of these alternatives, and, ultimately, to revise or reject the way of life their parents would pass down to them. This right applies both to the religious commitments and to the cultural mores of their home background. In Chapter Two I argue that they have a right to an education that will enable them to be self-sufficient participants in the economy they will enter as young adults; and that focusing on this right describes the limit to the obligation the school has to prepare children for the economy. That the economy needs more plumbers, or more software programmers, or more shopfloor greeters gives schools no reason to try and generate more people with suitable skills for those jobs. That children have a right to be self-supporting participants in the economy gives them a reason to prepare them for that. In Chapter Three I argue that children should be educated so that they can have rich and flourishing lives independently of their participation in the economy, and that this requires schools to focus more than some policymakers would like on what Americans think of as a liberal education, and Britons sometimes think of as an elitist academic curriculum. In Chapter Four, I argue that schools should educate children so that they can be effective, and reasonable, participants in public decisionmaking and execution. Broadly, children are well served both by having others who are reasonable and effective participants, and being able, when they become adults, to be reasonable and effective themselves. They are more likely to enjoy living in a just society, and more likely to be able to get their way when unjust measures are proposed against them.

Some of these principles will seem obvious to many readers; I hope that some will find them *all* obvious, but at least a few will find them all wrong. While I anticipate that many readers will be sympathetic (not least because people tend to read books they expect to find congenial), I should point out that especially the first two principles are much disputed, at least in public. Parents' rights lobbies insist that parents should have much more control than my first principle would allow over their children's moral development, and even that they should be able to shield them from alternatives to their own way of life. Many educators influenced by multiculturalism believe it is vital for children from ethnic minorities to be educated in a way that fits well with, and reinforces, the home culture. Some multiculturalists go as far as to claim that a child's home culture shapes what she is able to learn.

Similarly, politicians frequently argue that we should invest more in, or reform, education, for the sake of future economic growth. Employers complain that the education system does not meet their needs, and politicians listen (whether they act effectively to meet the employers' demands is another question). Developing countries do indeed have reasons to worry about future economic growth; but developed countries do not. Citizens of developed countries are surrounded by the fruits of a developed economy. These fruits are maldistributed, to be sure, but that problem is solvable in theory at least without further growth; and there is no serious prospect of long-term absolute decline. Students need the kind of education that will enable them to be effective participants in the economy, but there is no reason for states in developed countries to steer the education system towards the specific demands of employers.

My sense is that my third principle is less frequently disputed in public. But the third principle is in fact severely, and increasingly, neglected by policymakers. In the past 20 years a culture of testing, standards, and accountability has arisen in which it is easy to lose sight of the hard-to-test virtues of education for a rewarding life. I am much more well disposed to the practices of accountability than many educational theorists, and I do not think they are exclusively to blame for the fact that the intrinsic value of education has been neglected. The 1960s student activists who called for 'relevance' unleashed a monster that they could not control. Now it is the business community, and the politicians aligned with them, who make the same demand. But relevance to *what*? In pursuing relevance to the child's immediate surroundings and to the economy's short-term demands, we steer education away from the life-enhancing mission it could have. The child who develops at school a life-long love for poetry, or a fascination with history, or enthusiasm for abstract algebra, gets something vitally important even if it never serves her (or her future employers') economic goals. In Chapter Three I shall talk about what this principle means in practice for schooling, and shall argue in particular that schools need to emphasize the intrinsic value of intellectual pursuits to serve this end.

The fourth principle is, in one form or another, much touted by educationalists and politicians alike. Britain recently adopted 'citizenship' as a compulsory subject in the National Curriculum. Civics and social studies are returning to the curriculums of American schools, which also increasingly give credit for extra-curricular volunteering activities. Many States have recently renewed the demand that children learn to recite the Pledge of Allegiance in schools, and many school districts enforce a 'daily act of patriotic observance'. Chapter Four is about the goal of producing cooperative and reasonable citizens; what that goal amounts to and why it is legitimate. I shall say a little about the ways schools might reasonably attempt to do that; and I shall return to the topic in Chapter Six, where I shall argue that teaching patriotism is wrong and illegitimate.

The second part of the book takes up three concrete policy controversies in the light of the principles I have defended in the first part. Chapter Five deals with the increasingly vexing question on both sides of the Atlantic, of whether the state should fund religious schools. Although I adopt the kinds of principles that are usually associated with the anti-funding secularists (again, on both sides of the Atlantic), I argue that the funding arrangements in the UK (where religious schools are funded by the state) are more or less appropriate, and that the US would do well, in the light of my principles, to emulate whatever parts of those arrangements it can. In Chapter Six I look at the increased focus on using schooling to inculcate patriotism in children, and argue that doing so normally betrays some of the important and legitimate goals of education. Finally, in Chapter Seven, I look at the problems surrounding 'citizenship education'; which is a recent addition to the UK curriculum, though a standard part of most American public schools for many years (though not usually under that name). Citizenship education has been attacked in the UK as a kind of Trojan horse for state indoctrination. In fact the case for citizenship education is strong, but its opponents have some very reasonable fears about its implementation which schools, and teachers, should consider carefully in designing their approaches.

You'll have noticed that this is a short book, so I focus on what seem to me to be the crucial public questions about education on which I, as a practising philosopher who is well informed about both the world of education policy and the relevant evidence in the social sciences, have something to contribute. This strategy necessarily downplays some issues that some readers will think are more urgent. I always welcome suggestions of other issues to think about, and the reader can easily contact me through the Publisher to make suggestions for further work or criticisms of this one. But I do want to mention three gaps that will leap out to some readers.

First, although the book is called *On Education*, I focus much of the discussion on *schooling*. We all know that only part of a child's education occurs at school, while much else occurs in the home environment and in all sorts of informal ways outside the school. More complicatedly, what the school can and should contribute to education is influenced by what happens beyond the school. My own schooling was excellent, but a good deal of my education came from my parents, and a good deal more from BBC Radio 4. Friends of mine who were failed by school were educated within political movements, or through their churches or friendship networks. Why, then, should I focus on school, specifically?

I have several reasons. Most of the public debates about education, at least about the education of children, focus on schooling; and because I want this book to be a public engagement with current debates, I feel entitled to start where the public starts. But it is also true that modern wealthy societies expend a great deal of GDP on formal schooling of children. It is a worthwhile task to figure out what should be done with that money, given the impracticality of abolishing schooling. Most importantly, for me, schooling should not be abolished even if abolition were practical. Schooling is the only practical formal mechanism we have for guaranteeing (or trying to guarantee) that all children get reasonable access to education, regardless of how supportive their parents are of education. For most children, furthermore, certain aspects of education can only happen in a formal setting. Most children, including most children who come from homes that are well resourced and within which education is highly valued, will only learn higher forms of mathematics, foreign languages, and engagement with serious music and serious literature if they do so in a formal setting: school. Other aims of education, too, require schooling, or something structurally like it: most children need to interact with a reasonably wide variety of people in a formal and paternalistic setting in order to develop into autonomous persons and cooperative citizens, for example.

The second glaring omission is connected. I assume throughout that schooling will be compulsory for children up to the age of 16 or 18, or some other similar age. But why should we assume that? This question is motivated by two quite different considerations. The first is that schooling might be increasingly ineffective as children get older; especially for those children who do not aspire to academic achievement; it might seem cruel and/or wasteful to keep them in school beyond the age of 14 or, perhaps, 12. The second is a general distrust of paternalism towards children: some critics of compulsory schooling point out that children can take responsibility for caring for others, can achieve a great deal in paid work, and can become relevantly like 'responsible' adults at much earlier ages than most of us like to admit.

I have some sympathy with the first consideration. Despite enormous amounts of research and public effort, schools have not figured out how to do well by a good swathe of children from their early teens, and this is true even in countries that do not consign large percentages of children to growing up in conditions of poverty (as the US and the UK do). I do assume that schooling should be compulsory for younger children, but I adopt the assumption that it should be compulsory for all up to age 16 more for the sake of simplicity and argument than because I have a strong argument for it. But I will say that if schooling were able to achieve the goals outlined in this book, that this would constitute a powerful argument for making it compulsory to the later ages.

I have much less sympathy for the second consideration. I agree that children are able to do numerous things that adults do not readily trust them with at earlier ages. But there is an unacceptable opportunity cost to allowing them to do some of these things to the exclusion of formal education (as we would if we treated them as adults). Many skills and traits can only be acquired in childhood; others are learned much more efficiently in childhood than later in life. Think of language learning. If you have not learned a first language by the age of 7, you never will. If you have not learned a second by the age of 18 you still might, but it will be much more difficult than if you learn it earlier, and you will (almost certainly) never speak it without an accent. If we allow children to engage in numerous weekly hours of paid work, or allow them to be primary carers for ailing parents or other children, we interfere with their prospects for acquiring the skills and traits which underpin a flourishing life in wealthy modern societies. This is true even if they are entirely competent workers and carers, and even if they would prefer to be engaged in that kind of activity. We owe a duty to children that their childhood be rich and enjoyable, but we also owe them a duty to prepare them so that they can have a significant range of opportunities to lead a flourishing life in adulthood. The first part of the book can be seen as an argument for this duty, and as filling out what the duty consists of.

The third glaring omission concerns the distribution of educational opportunities. A great deal of public debate in both the UK and the US concerns educational inequality: to what extent is it just for some children to have better educational opportunities than others? Which sources of educational inequality are legitimate, and which sources are unjust? I have said a great deal about these and related questions in other publications, and the need for brevity and focus has here overcome the will for completeness![1]

You don't need any background in philosophy to read this book; you only need to have spent 10 or so years in school and have thought about what was going on around you. It is written mainly for readers who are interested in education, and have wondered about the questions raised: what is the point of schooling, and how should schools be organized in the light of that? I hope that my fellow professional philosophers and educationists will learn something from it, but it is not written primarily for them.

I have drawn my examples and concerns almost exclusively from two countries: the US and the UK. This will annoy some readers, but I have done it for two reasons. First modesty: I know both countries and their education systems well, and know no others well at all, and have a certain reluctance to write about things I don't know about. Second, because the two systems are very different, and therefore make for good contrasts. The issues in the book arise in very different ways in the two countries, and focusing on them both will therefore make it easier, not more difficult, for readers from other countries to figure out how to apply the considerations in their own national contexts.

Because I have drawn my examples and issues from the US and the UK, I should make the obligatory comment on linguistic preferences. Where American and British English differ, I have usually preferred American usage; so 'pupils' are 'students', 'state schools' are 'public schools' and 'primary school' is 'elementary school'. The one exception is that I use 'secondary school' to refer to secondary school or, in American terms, the grades that are included in middle and high schools. I've done this not out of any general preference for American usage, but because the American terms in each case fit better with the ordinary language meanings of the terms, and are gaining currency in other Anglophone countries, including the UK.

Part One
Educational Aims

One

Consider the following case. The Amish constitute an enclosed religious community in some mid-Western and Eastern States. They live fairly separately from the rest of American society; they don't pay taxes or take benefits from the state, they spurn many of the new technologies that other Americans take for granted; they do not watch television or drive motor cars. They do trade with outsiders to a limited extent, but they are reasonably close to constituting a self-sufficient community. In the early 1970s a group of Amish in my home state of Wisconsin challenged a law requiring that all children be subject to some formal schooling up until the age of 16. The Amish litigants claimed that such a requirement violated their right to freedom of conscience, because during the early teen years, children are especially vulnerable to secular influences, so subjecting children of that age to formal education jeopardizes their belief in God and, ultimately, their opportunity for salvation.

The case, known as *Yoder v. Wisconsin*, went to the US Supreme Court. The Court found against the State of Wisconsin, and the school-leaving age for Amish children was reduced to 14. Because the Amish constitute a quasi-separate society, and because the Amish children would not become a drain on the State as a result of their lack of education (since very few leave, and those who remain do not take government assistance), the State was said to have no compelling interest in forcing them to be educated.

What seems wrong with this decision? At least some readers will worry that children who are raised within an enclosed community, in which everyone worships the same God in the same way, and from which exit is possible only at the cost of being shunned, will be forced into ways of life that do not suit them. Others will worry that those children will not acquire the skills and information needed for them to make their own judgements about whether the way of life their community expects them to adopt is a good one for them. It may, indeed, be excellent for some of those children. However, even for those children, something is lost if they adopt the life without having reflected on it in the light of alternatives.

The key problem is that the children appear to be deprived of the opportunity to make and act on well-informed and well-thought out judgements about how to live their own lives. In practice, the only feasible way of life for them is the one in which they were raised, whether it suits them or not. In other words, they are deprived of the opportunity to live autonomously.

But why should that matter so much? Many philosophers have thought of autonomy as the key to a good life. Socrates famously said that 'only the examined life is worth living'. Immanuel Kant, the moral philosopher whose theories underlie a great deal of contemporary liberal thinking, believed that only the autonomous person could act in ways that had moral worth. But, of course, this is precisely what the Amish parents dispute. They believe that a good and moral life is one lived in accord with the commands of God, regardless of whether the individual's judgement is made in awareness of a wide range of alternatives. And many secular defenders of the Yoder decision accuse its opponents of failing to recognize the importance of many other values than autonomy. The Amish children will not be fully autonomous in the secular sense, perhaps, but they will enjoy the goods of participating in a close-knit community; they will see their parents and children almost every day of their lives; they will experience close and lasting emotional attachments. These are tremendous goods, which would be threatened by a more demanding education policy. Who, the defenders of the decision say, are you to elevate autonomy over these other goods?

In this opening chapter I shall argue that autonomy is important enough to justify a requirement that all children be subject to an education designed to facilitate it. But I am going to do so without claiming that autonomy is needed for a life to be worth living. So my argument for facilitating autonomy has to be grounded in a deeper principle that explains why it is so important.

This deeper principle is the idea that education should aim at enabling people to lead flourishing lives, and the argument that education should facilitate autonomy depends on the idea that autonomy plays an important role in enabling people to live flourishing lives. There are many different ways for people to flourish, and people vary in what kinds of life they will be able to flourish within. But flourishing lives have two things in common. First, for a life to be truly worthwhile, it must contain objective goods. However much a miser enjoys his hoarding, his life is not made worthwhile by it, because a life devoted to hoarding money is not worthwhile. But lives devoted to raising children, mastering difficult and complex skills, giving enjoyment to others and enjoying their company, studying great literature, devising great comic routines, can be worthwhile lives because they contain *objectively valuable goods*. I don't have space here to defend any particular view of what makes something objectively valuable (although I say more about flourishing in Chapter Three) and any list of objective goods will be somewhat controversial. Still, it is not very controversial that there exists a wide variety of goods, nor that there is a basis for distinguishing them from, at least some, very bad things.

So far the defender of the Yoder decision doesn't have to disagree. In fact, part of impetus behind support for that decision is the recognition that although their way of life is alien to mainstream American society, it is not, by virtue of that fact, bad. But having objectively good things in one's life is not enough for a flourishing life. For somebody actually to flourish, they have to identify with the life they are leading. They have to live it from the inside, as it were. Now someone can know that their way of life suits them well without knowing or thinking much about alternatives, so they don't have to think critically about the alternatives in order to identify with their life. But they must, at the very least, not experience their way of life as being at odds with their most fundamental experienced interests and desires.

Both components – that the way of life is good, and that it is lived from the inside – are essential. Some ways of life are not good, and children whose parents pass them down cannot live them well even if they endorse them: those children have no opportunity to live well unless they are able to find good ways of life. Other ways of life are, of course, good. But some whose parents try to pass those ways of life down cannot endorse them from the inside: although the ways of life are good, these people cannot flourish within them. They have opportunities to live well only if they can enter other good ways of life which they *are* able to endorse from the inside. How able they are to exit into a good way of life depends, partly, on whether they possess reliable ways of evaluating different ways of life.

Why might some people be unable to live some good ways of life from the inside? First, people's personalities vary on numerous dimensions: exuberance; spontaneity; gregariousness; how much they find their fulfilment in their work and how much in their personal relationships. Some of these differences are, no doubt, socially constructed, and some lie within the control of the individual. But not all. Some people just could not be fulfilled without their work (or some work); others could not be fulfilled without having children. We cannot design children's upbringings to achieve some desired set of traits.

The plurality of personal constitutions is important: some persons' constitutions will allow them to live some ways of life from the inside, but not others. The starkest case I can think of concerns people who experience their sexuality as fixed and unadaptable. A homosexual who experiences his homosexuality as unchangeable simply cannot live, from the inside, a way of life in which those who refrain from heterosexual marriage and childrearing are social outsiders. Trapped in such a way of life, he will be alienated from it. It may be a very good way of life, but it is not one that *he* can endorse from the inside, and is therefore not one that *he* can live well. Similarly, some religious ways of life which impose on women the duties of fidelity in marriage and modesty conflict with the natures of some women who are raised in those religions. Take the character Sonia Horowitz in the film *A Price Above Rubies*. An orthodox Jew, she marries a young scholar as a teenager. He becomes much revered for his scholarly and spiritual life, but as he develops it he neglects her both emotionally and sexually. Now, there may well be some women who could be comfortable living modestly as the wife of a saint for their whole lives, and there is nothing to suggest that there would be anything wrong with their lives. But for Sonia, *with her particular constitution*, it would be impossible to continue such a life and endorse it from within, even if she were unaware of alternatives.

Different ways of life elevate different virtues, and some children are ill constituted to develop the particular virtues that their parents' way of life endorses. Some children will, of course, be well suited to the ways of life into which they are inducted by their parents. But neither the state nor their parents can identify these children in advance. So to guarantee that all children have the opportunity to live well, the state must ensure that all children have a real opportunity to enter good ways of life other than those into which their parents seek to induct them.

What does it take to provide a child with the opportunity to enter other ways of life than that of her parents? We are properly reluctant to have the state comment on the substantive ends of citizens, and tend to focus instead on the provision of resources and liberties to citizens. But if someone has all the resources and liberties that justice requires, but has, as an avoidable result of the design of social institutions, hardly any opportunity to live well, she has not been treated justly. One purpose of delivering the resources and liberties that justice requires is to enable people to live well by their own judgement. But to live well, one needs more: one also needs some sense of what constitutes living well. So providing the opportunity to enter ways of life requires that the state educate children in the skills of rational reflection and comparison usually associated with autonomy.

Were learning how to live well an entirely mysterious matter, or if equipping people with the skills associated with learning how to live well conflicted with other elements of justice, it might be conceded that justice requires only the delivery of external resources and conditions. But the basic methods of rational evaluation are reliable aids to uncovering how to live well, and they are the only such aids that can be identified and taught. This is especially important in modern conditions, with 'fast changing technologies and free movement of labour [which calls for] an ability to cope with changing technological, economic and social conditions, for an ability to adjust, to acquire new skills, to move from one subculture to another, to come to terms with new scientific and moral views.'[1] Without autonomy-related skills we are easily lost in the moral and economic complexity of modernity. This does not imply that no-one will hit upon, or at least approach, good ways of life without their aid, nor that rational deliberation is infallible. As in other areas of knowledge, inspired guesses, trusting the reliable communication of another, and manipulation by reliable others, can help us to discover how to live well. And rational deliberation confronts barriers. But in the absence of fortunate guesses and well-informed parents, children will be much better placed to enter alternative good ways of life if they are well informed about alternatives and are able rationally to compare them.

The conception of autonomy I am invoking may seem both abstract and self-absorbed. In fact it is neither. Autonomy has a deeply social aspect, not least because human beings are deeply social beings. Individuals do not flourish separately from others; their interests are bound up with those of other people, and their reflection takes place within a given social context. Certainly they subject both their own personal traits and the relationships within their situation to rational scrutiny. Rational reflection can help us to detect inconsistencies and fallacious argumentation, and to uncover misuse of evidence. It helps us to see whether a choice coheres with our given judgements, including our judgements about what kind of person we ought to be. It also helps us to evaluate the ways we are attached to other people, and to carry out our altruistic obligations and goals more effectively. Careful reflection on moral matters, for example, might lead us to believe that we have much more extensive obligations to the needy than unreflective acceptance of the norms in our immediate environment would suggest to us; or it might lead us to realize that pursuit of promotion comes at unacceptable cost to our local friendships or family life. It is also important to notice that rational reflection can, and often does, lead us to affirm our existing traits, values, commitments, and attachments.

These observations support a strong presumption that children should have the opportunity to learn the skills associated with autonomy and that parental preference is not sufficient reason to deny them that opportunity. In waiving the opportunity, parents would be depriving their children of skills which are of great value in working out how to live well. Does the argument, though, support intervention in the life of the school?

I think this depends on certain contingencies. Imagine a child growing up in a society characterized by a culture which affords abundant public models of the relevant skills, and in which respectful engagement with people from quite different backgrounds was the norm. Politicians in this society engage with each other's best arguments; members of different religious communities openly debate and discuss their differences, and although they worship separately they mingle socially; journalists engage critically and in a well-informed way with public policy proposals; popular culture is diverse and not dominated by the profit motive. In such a society, it might be a complete waste of public resources to facilitate autonomy through schooling; civil society does such a good job of it already that schools would be free to pursue other excellences.

The public cultures of the US and the UK both fall somewhat short of this ideal, sufficiently short, I think, that we are justified in calling on schools to play a role in facilitating autonomy.

How, though, should schools achieve autonomy-facilitation? Think of school authorities as having power over three aspects of school life. They can determine the composition of the school, the curriculum, and the ethos. All three of these are probably important, and they work together. However, I suspect that the composition of the school and the ethos are more important than the formal curriculum. We probably learn more about how different ways of life are articulated, and about whether they would be well suited for us, through encounters with other people who live differently from us. An autonomy-facilitating school will be composed of both children and adults who come from a diversity of backgrounds, and who have differing outlooks on the world and how to live their lives. A school with Muslim, Hindu, atheist, Roman Catholic, and Jewish children will do better, other things being equal, than one in which all the children are Roman Catholic. A school in which the teachers have a variety of faiths and ethnic backgrounds, and between them display a diversity of personal enthusiasms, will do better than one in which they are all cut from the same cloth.

The goal of autonomy-facilitation makes diversity desirable for very different reasons than are usually given in arguments about diversity in education. A standard argument for diversity among school employees is that it should match the diversity of the students, so that each child has some teachers or other authority figures whose background matches their own, and with whom they can therefore identify. That is not the argument here at all: I am suggesting that we should seek diversity among the employees precisely so that each child has some authority figures who are quite different, and whom he or she will have to relate to. Autonomy-facilitation requires a modicum of discontinuity between the child's home experience and her school experience, so that the opportunities provided by the home (and the public culture) are supplemented, rather than replicated, in the school.

The ethos of that school will encourage genuine and serious engagement between the children, and between them and the adults, in an atmosphere that is emotionally stable and physically safe. The aim is not to promote *toleration* between different groups (though that, too, is important) but to enable children to learn more about alternative ways of living and new perspectives. These are resources for the children, which enable them to reflect critically on opinions and values received from their families and from the mainstream culture. Achieving an ethos which facilitates such mutual learning is difficult, and in a short book I am mercifully spared the obligation to say much about it. But two comments are worth making. First, notice that children from ethnic and religious minorities already, when they come to school, experience a potentially fruitful discontinuity between their home environment and the public culture. And they are more likely than children from the ethnic majority to encounter teachers who are different from them. It may be a good deal harder to achieve an autonomy-facilitating environment for children whose home environment fits well with the public culture.

Second, whereas my example of the Amish might suggest that religious parenting is the central threat to personal autonomy, I doubt that is the case, precisely because most children from religious backgrounds will routinely have their home values challenged by the public culture. Much more troubling for the vast majority of children is a public, and particularly a popular, culture that is governed by commercial forces, that dedicate considerable resources to undermining children's prospective autonomy, aiming to inculcate a life-long and unreflective materialism in as many children as possible.[2] The school administrator concerned with developing an autonomy-facilitating ethos will constantly question the potential effects of allowing the school to reflect the values embodied in popular culture.

I'll develop these comments about composition and ethos a little further in Chapter Five. Finally in this chapter, though, it is worth noting some of the curricular elements that autonomy-facilitation suggests.

- The traditional academic, content-based curriculum. Proponents of teaching critical thinking skills and autonomy in the curriculum often sound as if they are opposing the traditional emphasis on teaching 'facts' and 'content' in the curriculum. But there is no real conflict here: an autonomous life cannot be led without the information about the world in which it is led. Furthermore, the critical thinking skills involved in autonomy can neither be developed nor exercised without the ease of access to a considerable amount of information which is provided only by having learned and internalized it. It is true that there is far more information available than any child can be expected to learn, and that it is crucial that children learn how to get access to information. However, the idea that they might develop the more complex skills of reasoning about information without having a good deal of it instantly available is silly.[3]

- How to identify various sorts of fallacious arguments, and how to distinguish among them, as well as between them and non-fallacious arguments. The autonomous person needs to be able to distinguish between appeals to authority and appeals to evidence, between inductive and deductive arguments, as well as to identify ad hominem arguments and other misleading rhetorical devices.
- About a range of religious, non-religious, and anti-religious ethical views in some detail, about the kinds of reasoning deployed within those views, and the attitudes of proponents towards non-believers, heretics, and the secular world.
- About the diverse ways (including non-reason-based ways) in which secular and religious thinkers have dealt with moral conflict and religious disagreements, and with tensions in their own views; and how individuals have described (and to the extent possible how they have experienced) conversion experiences, losses of faith, and reasoned abandonment of ethical positions.

These last two elements are particularly important, since autonomy with respect to one's religious and moral commitments requires exposure to alternative views. It also requires that this exposure be done in a controlled and non-pressured way, but also in a way that reflects the reality of the lives lived according to these commitments. Exposure to moral views would occur best by allowing proponents of views to address children in the controlled environment of the classroom. While the instrumental argument is connected to the liberal humanism which is anathema to many religious sectarians, the implementation of autonomy-facilitating education would probably require a nuanced attitude to the exposure of children to religion in schools. A child cannot be autonomous either in her acceptance or rejection of a religious view unless she experiences serious advocacy. As John Stuart Mill argues, concerning the exposure of adults to free speech:

> Nor is it enough that he should hear the arguments of adversaries from his own teachers, presented as they state them, and accompanied by what they offer as refutations. That is not the way to do justice to the arguments, or bring them into real contact with his own mind. He must be able to hear them from persons who actually believe them; who defend them in earnest and do their very utmost for them.[4]

Neutral, antiseptic textbooks describing each view and serially explaining its advantages and defects may contribute little to autonomy-facilitation – they certainly would not suffice. Autonomy, though susceptible of an abstract description, cannot be practised outside the specific situation of individual lives; schools should reflect this.

Suppose we inculcate in a child the skills and habits associated with autonomy. Does this guarantee to them the ability to live flourishing life? Absolutely not. For that they need far more: they need to access to material resources, and some control over their worklife; they need to be able to adopt a way of life that is itself good; and they need an environment in which they can act on their judgements. The subsequent three chapters explore these needs.

Two

Since the end of the Cold War a new consensus seems to have emerged among Western governments that education provides the key to growth and competitiveness. The idea is that since labour is a major factor of production, better labour will be more productive, and what makes for better labour is education and training. Just as a better screwdriver enables you to be more productive (if your job involves screwdrivers), so more skilled workers will make the economy more productive. A pamphlet produced by the British Labour Party just before it won the 1997 election expresses the idea well:

> If we are to face the challenge of creating a high tech, high added value and high wage economy, we can only do so by skilling our people.[1]

This is called the human capital theory approach; the imperative is developing a strong and competitive economy, and the means is educating children to be productive workers. This benefits everyone; we all gain from higher Gross Domestic Product, and children gain from the fact that they are more able to operate well in the workplace.

Although it is highly influential among policymakers, I think the human capital theory approach is mistaken. Of course, it is true that better educated workers are often more productive, and that is not necessarily a bad thing. But economic growth should not be the imperative behind education provision, at least in the compulsory years. Moreover, in particular, the content and distribution of educational opportunities should not be tailored to the interests of employers.

Remember, at the core of the argument for autonomy is the idea that schooling should equip us to live a flourishing life. In modern industrial societies people need to be able to integrate themselves to a certain degree in the existing economy in order to flourish. In this chapter I'm going to argue that while schools do have an obligation to ensure that children can be economically self-sufficient, they should not try to fit their mission to the needs of the economy as a whole. The schools should orient themselves to the needs of the children who will have to deal with the economy, and not to the needs of the economy itself.

Of course, if the education system failed completely to take account of the economy, it would be failing the children it purported to serve. But this is true only because schools have an obligation to prepare children to be able to flourish in the society they will inhabit. Teaching children ancient weaving techniques, and restricting their education to such arcane skills, runs the risk that they will be unemployable when they enter the economy. This matters, not because they would then be unable to contribute to a social project of promoting economic production, but because for most of us paid employment is necessary in order for us to flourish. We all need an income, and we almost all need a sense that some of that income is generated, in part, by our own efforts. I shall argue against prioritizing the needs of the economy after I have argued that schools should develop children's capacities for economic self-reliance.

Three main considerations support the requirement to prepare children for the world of work. Obviously people need an income to flourish. In a market economy we need to be able to pay for the basic necessities of life, without which we cannot enjoy our lives. For most of us in most market economies, the only way of getting an income large enough to provide a measure of security is by working for a wage. But that is not the only reason that schools should prepare children for the world of work. A second reason is that work, for most people, consumes a sizeable part of their lives. What happens at work affects their sense of wellbeing. Having a wider rather than a narrower range of skills, including the skills to negotiate with supervisors and co-workers in the workplace, increases their power over what will happen to them there, and hence their ultimate wellbeing. Finally, people appear to need a sense that they, themselves, are responsible for their own income and subsequent wellbeing; they need not just income but a sense of self-reliance.

The need for income in a market economy is obvious, and does not require further elaboration. But the human capital approach will equip most people to earn an income. Suppose, for a moment, that a generous basic income grant were in place, so that anyone who so desired could live at a Spartan subsistence level without working. Should schools still prepare children for economic self-sufficiency?

Yes. Income is not the only valuable reward that work brings. People also attain status through their work, both in the competitive sense that social respect is distributed unequally among occupations, and in the self-regarding sense that people think of themselves differently as paid workers than if they are unemployed. Cultures differ in how they distribute respect across occupations and in how they prepare people to regard themselves as workers. To give a stark example, the recently formed social expectation that women spend most of their adult lives in paid employment has probably affected the way that women who opt out of the paid workplace in favour of domestic labour regard themselves and their choice, as well as affecting the actual content of their choice. It is quite different to stay at home to raise a child when half the women in the neighbourhood are doing the same thing from opting for this choice when no others are doing so.

People also flourish at work, if they are lucky enough to have work that they find interesting and an environment in which they have some control over what they do and when. Fortunately, people vary in what they find interesting. For example, Sid finds the sight of blood sickening, and has very little interest in people, so he'd find being a family doctor something akin to torture; however, he is thrilled by the challenge of flying an airliner. Ken has a fear of flying, but enjoys company and problem-solving with people. A good deal of research suggests that people flourish primarily through engagement with family and friends, but work can provide a diversity of challenges and rewards that can sometimes compete with, and sometimes enhance, the fulfilment of personal relationships. So the general principle that everyone should have a wide set of opportunities to flourish supports educating them so that they have the opportunity to find rewarding work, and can judge the relative importance of work and other activities in their lives.[2]

Even under the regime of a generous basic income grant, most households would want to have at least the equivalent of one adult in full-time work. Given the existence of the grant, it is true, workplaces would have to make themselves more appealing to workers, and the consequences of dismissal would be much less catastrophic than in our current economies. Still, workers who stay in a single workplace for a long time have less bargaining power. They make friends there, live in a neighbourhood from which they can access the workplace relatively easily, and, especially if the local economy has limited demand for their skills, seeking another job is disruptive. Coming into the labour market with a wider rather than a narrower range of skills gives young adults more choice about what kinds of work to accept, and enables them to opt for more intrinsically rewarding rather than less rewarding labour, as well as giving them more scope in making trade-offs between higher pay and greater intrinsic rewards.

The final reason that education should prepare children for employment is that many people seem to need some sense that they are economically self-reliant, at least over the course of their lives. Self-respect is bolstered by the sense that one is pulling one's weight, rather than free-riding on the efforts of others. This was a major motivation behind demands from feminists that labour markets should open up to women. It is now a central motivation behind calls in the disability movement that companies not be allowed to discriminate against people with disabilities, and that they should have to alter the physical space of the workplace to accommodate the physically impaired.

It is worth remembering that there is something artificial about anyone's sense of self-reliance. We tend to think of ourselves as deserving our salary, whatever that salary is, and our sense of self-reliance rests on this thought. But, in fact, our salaries, and even the kinds of job available to us, are a consequence of a multiplicity of choices and decisions over which we had no control, and which could have been different. Tiger Woods enjoys a much higher income than he would have enjoyed, even in an advanced economy, if television had never been invented, or if it had been invented but had been regulated everywhere to prohibit advertising. Top soccer players now enjoy much higher incomes relative to the population than they did 40 years ago. This is partly because the rest of the population has much larger disposable incomes (which it chooses to spend on watching soccer) but also because of major changes in labour market regulation over which they had no control (for example, the erosion of the ability of national sports leagues to limit employment of foreign players). It has very little to do with any increase in natural talent. In particular cases, the size of someone's salary can depend simply on the presence or absence of a particular rival. Remaining with sport, take the example of Steffi Graff, whose income doubled between 1992 and 1993, because she started winning, rather than coming second, in the major tennis tournaments. She had not improved her performance at all; Monica Seles, her main rival, left the tournament after being stabbed by a deranged fan. Graff would not claim that she was responsible for her improved situation, but there is every chance that she felt that she deserved the increased income.

The Graff/Seles example is stark because they were at the very top end of a winner-take-all labour market. But all of us operate in a world over which we have limited control, and in which the amount we earn depends on other people's preferences, judgements, and decisions, as much as, if not more than, our own efforts and talents. The artificiality of our incomes, and the conditions of our lives, go deep. We are not literally self-reliant, and it cannot literally be the case that we all put in as much as we take out, as it were; nor can we always tell the true value of what we are producing/consuming.

Furthermore, the probability that we will be net producers is affected by the design of the economy and social system. So, for example, dyslexics have a better chance of being net producers in pre-literate economies than in advanced ones: and also a better chance in economies in which dyslexia has been well studied. Consider someone with a very common, and disabling, disease. Because the disabling disease is common there are economic, and utilitarian, reasons to devote more resources to studying it and it is therefore more likely that an ultimately inexpensive treatment or cure will be found. The person who suffers from such a condition is more likely than someone who suffers an intrinsically equally disabling condition to be able to become a full participant in society, and the workforce, and is therefore more likely to enjoy the sense of self-reliance which I say is so important. Among the ordinarily-abled, different talents receive different rewards in different societies, and at different stages of economic development; and there is nothing much that we as individuals can do to alter that.

So the sense of self-reliance is, to a considerable extent, socially constructed. But the need for it is nevertheless real, and for most of us it is hard to maintain that sense without having paid employment for a substantial part of our lives. In societies that lack a generous basic income grant it is essential, for other reasons, to prepare children for the world of work. But even if it were possible for many people to enjoy a decent standard of living without paid employment, we should prepare them all so that they could take up paid employment if they wanted to.

What does equipping a child for paid employment require in practice? Answers to this question will vary by context. The skills and knowledge needed to earn a decent salary in a largely agricultural economy are somewhat different from those needed in a largely industrial economy; and those are different again from those needed in a 'post-industrial' economy. The structure of job ladders also affects what skills and knowledge it is appropriate for schooling to inculcate. The breakdown of the apprentice system, and abandonment by most industries of responsibility for training in the 1960s and 1970s in the UK, for example, placed greater demands on the formal education system than it had experienced previously.

Schools should not, though, think of themselves as preparing pupils to fit any particular 'slot' in the economy. Every child has a right to expect that her education will prepare her for a range of different kinds of employment. So equipping a child for the labour market requires teaching them the 'basics' – they should be literate, have reasonably good mathematical skills, have learned at least one foreign language, and know something of the sciences. They should also understand something of the way in which the labour market works, and of what their rights and responsibilities as an employee will be. This latter requirement imposes an important constraint on the design of vocational education curriculums. Most young people will enter the labour force as employees, rather than as employers. They will learn a great deal from their employers about what their responsibilities are, and, probably, somewhat less about what their rights are. Explicitly vocational education curriculums therefore need to emphasize the rights of employees. Ironically, as union membership has declined in the US, official curriculums are less likely to do this, because employers' organizations have more weight in the bodies which determine standards. So schools are obliged to scrutinize the official curriculums and ensure that they are properly meeting the real interests of the students.

In both the US and the UK something close to 50 per cent of school-leavers do not enter the workforce permanently, but enter higher education first. Given the high rate of higher education uptake and the benefits that higher education yields for those who undertake it, schools are obliged to prepare children to be competitive for college entrance. This vindicates a great deal of the traditional academic curriculum (as, I shall argue in the next chapter, does the imperative to prepare children for their lives), since performance in this part of the curriculum is important for college entrance. But most college students will spend a fair amount of the early adulthood as employees, albeit employees with a wide array of options.

That is the case for equipping children for paid employment. Now, why, in the light of the fact that we have an obligation to do that, is it wrong for us to infuse the education system with the imperatives of the economy?

There are two main reasons for this. To explain the first, I shall have to make some rather unrealistic assumptions; in particular that we can know exactly what policies will produce a given level of growth. Relaxing this assumption itself strengthens the case against following the imperatives of the economy; because we are not well informed about what effect education policies have on growth, we do well to avoid making strong assumptions that may well be false. But let's assume full information for a moment. Suppose that an economy faces the following two options:

- **Option A:** long-term growth at 7 per cent per annum in the foreseeable future, which will be generated if we ensure that 30 per cent of workers are well prepared for dull, unrewarding work in the service sector, whereas the other 70 per cent are prepared for intellectually interesting and well-paid work.

- **Option B:** long-term growth of just 1 per cent per annum in the foreseeable future, the lost growth being a cost incurred for the policy of educating everyone so that they will be able to pursue a variety of interesting employment opportunities, with the result that the 30 per cent of low-wage service sector jobs that drive growth are either left unfilled or have to raise their wages in a way that depresses growth.

I think that if we really faced these two options, Option B would be preferable. Restricting the education of some children simply for the sake of long-term growth of the economy, in an economy that is not impoverished, is wrong, and it is wrong for distributive reasons; it constitutes using those people for the sake of others, and without any compensating benefit accruing to them.

Of course, I have made unrealistic economic assumptions in designing the example, as well as unrealistic assumptions about our knowledge. And, in fact, some level of economic growth is compatible with an education system that is designed to meet the other imperatives I am endorsing in this book. Furthermore, wealth matters. If pursuit of the imperatives I am endorsing in the education system would result in the economic collapse of some society, then that would count against pursuing them in those circumstances, precisely because that collapse would be very bad for the least advantaged people in the society. But the point here is that, absent catastrophic consequences for the economy, these child-centred imperatives should dominate any economic criterion.

The objection can, perhaps, be illuminated by considering

the following statement from a World Bank education strategy paper, which supports prioritizing the education of women and girls in developing countries.

> Mothers with more education provide better nutrition to their children, have healthier children, are less fertile, and are more concerned that their children be educated. Education – in particular female education – is key to reducing poverty and must be considered as much part of a country's health strategy as, say, programs of immunization and access to health clinics.[3]

This is true, and it does constitute one reason to educate girls (and hence produce educated mothers). There is ample evidence that women with better education are more concerned with their children's education and better able to manage their children's health and development. Educating girls better must be part of any strategy for the reduction of poverty and improvement in the quality of life in the developing world. But notice that the statement focuses exclusively on the benefits that educating any particular girl has for other people. The passage I have quoted treats the girl as a vassal for the imperatives of the economy; educate her to benefit others and produce much-needed economic growth. But the central point of educating someone is for her own benefit; that it will enable her to live a more rewarding life over which she will have more control. Of course, if the goal of universal primary education is achieved, it will have the effect of improving women's lives both because they will gain from the consequent reduction in poverty and because they will have directly benefited from the education they receive. But the human capital theory approach which currently finds favour, although it contains an important truth, obscures another, which is that the person being educated matters in her own right.

The second objection to letting the desire for economic growth guide the education system may be more controversial. This objection says that, once a society has achieved a certain level of material wellbeing, further growth is not fundamentally very important. So neither should education policy, nor should other aspects of government policy, be dominated by the imperative of economic growth. This objection holds that the good we should be trying to produce for society is not economic growth, but human flourishing, and there are better ways of increasing the level of flourishing than by increasing material wealth.

This contradicts the consensus among politicians and policymakers and, of course, businesspeople (whose organizations have considerable influence over policy making). Both left- and right-wing politicians participate in the consensus for growth. Since the 1970s, left-wing parties in the developed, and increasingly the developing world, look to growth as the way of solving the problem of maldistribution. The 'class war', which involved a struggle over the distribution of existing assets, has been abandoned for a strategy of trying to skew the distribution of the fruits of economic growth towards the least advantaged. For this strategy to work, there has to be a good deal of growth. Right-wing politicians like growth because they think that material wealth underpins a successful society. The left-wing strategy may have something going for it, but the right-wing view is open to dispute. The evidence simply does not support the idea that, above a certain level, material wealth translates into human flourishing.

Two kinds of study undermine the idea that material wellbeing translates directly into flourishing. One kind of study looks at changes in average levels of subjective well-being over time within given societies, and asks how well those changes correlate with economic growth. The second kind looks at distribution of subjective wellbeing within a society at a given time, and asks how well that correlates with the distribution of income and wealth. Both kinds of study measure 'subjective wellbeing' by using complex surveys, administered to large populations of individuals. Of course, subjective wellbeing is a very crude measure of something as complex and contested as human flourishing. The results of these kinds of study are, though, supported by smaller-scale experimental studies which consider objective measures such as stress-response, headaches, anxiety, and depression. Since my claim is only that the evidence does not support the consensus, I think it is worth looking at the results of the studies.

The wellbeing-over-time studies find that, within developed economies, there is no increase in average subjective wellbeing once growth reaches a certain point. Between 1972 and 1991 real GDP per capita grew in the US, at a more or less steady rate, by 39 per cent. The percentage of respondents to polls reporting themselves as 'very happy' barely increased at all during the same period; and the kinks in that curve bear no relationship to the steady rise in the growth curve.[4] In Japan, GNP per capita grew steadily from 1960 to 1987 by a total of 300 per cent; the average reported level of wellbeing in reported by respondents to surveys changed barely at all year to year, hovering around 6 (out of 10).[5] Robert Frank summarizes the evidence as follows:

> One of the central findings in the large scientific literature on subjective well-being is that once income levels surpass a

> minimal absolute threshold, average satisfaction levels
> within a given country tend to be highly stable over time, even
> in the face of significant economic growth.[6]

It is not that wealth has no bearing on wellbeing. In fact, in both the UK and the US, the proportions of people describing themselves as 'very happy' or 'happy' rise, consistently, with material growth, until about the mid-1950s. But after that there is no gain.

The wellbeing/income studies, similarly, find that once annual income exceeds a certain level, levels of subjective wellbeing are unaffected by income. In the United States, for example, subjective wellbeing grows with income up to a (quite high) annual household income of about $200,000 a year, and after that it stops. And we cannot increase subjective wellbeing just by raising everyone's incomes to at least $200,000, because the evidence strongly suggests that as long as the economic pie is big enough (as it is in the rich countries of the world today), one's relative place in the distribution of the existing pie matters a great deal more for one's level of subjective wellbeing than one's absolute level of material wellbeing. Only once one has achieved a very high place in the distribution, and the material security and the control over one's work and social environment that accompanies that, does the relative effect disappear. If this is true, it goes some way to vindicating the now abandoned 'class war' strategy of trying to redistribute the existing pie more equally.

These findings chime with Fred Hirsch's argument in *Social Limits to Growth* that, past a certain point of material development, as the material economy grows, what he calls the *positional* economy becomes an increasingly dominant part of the material economy.[7] The positional economy relates to certain kinds of goods that cannot be more widely distributed, because their value lies in the social construction of their high status, and part of that status rests on the fact that access to these goods is limited. Status, itself, is a positional good. Hirsch worries that in wealthy societies, a great deal of human energy and effort is wasted in the competition for positional goods, especially if the competition for these goods is designed as a high-stakes competition (in which the winners are few and very successful, and the losers are many). The competition is wasteful in the sense it diverts people's resources from other, much more intrinsically rewarding, activities and pursuits.

If this is correct, then growth is only desirable in so far as people get more real value (in terms of personal flourishing) from it. The best way, in wealthy societies, for people to get more flourishing from growth in productivity is for it to provide them with more leisure time: more time to spend with family and friends; more time to spend on labour which is unpaid and intrinsically rewarding; more time to be free from the stress that comes from other people having power over them. The best way to promote human flourishing at the current levels of wealth in wealthy societies is not to increase the amount of wealth, but to redistribute it, and to use it to underwrite leisure. Given this fact, even if we knew how to design schooling to promote growth (which we don't), we'd do better to use schooling to enable children to interact with the economy in ways that facilitate their flourishing in their leisure time. It is to this proposition that I shall devote the next chapter.

Three

The key idea in this book is that the central purpose of education is to promote human flourishing. At the foundation of the arguments for preparing children to be autonomous and preparing them for the labour market is the idea that these are extremely valuable in order for them to be able to live flourishing lives. The school should see itself as having an obligation to facilitate the long-term flourishing of the children. In this chapter, I want to discuss the more direct implication that this requirement has: that schools should prepare children to lead flourishing lives.

Some readers will already be uncomfortable with this. Who are we, they might say, to presume to know what will make for a flourishing life for someone else? What gives me the right to impose my view of how they will flourish on them? Teachers, especially, might baulk at the paternalistic role this suggests for them.

I have some sympathy with this strand of opinion, but only some. At its limit, it calls into question the very idea of parental obligation. If I feel uncomfortable with the role of facilitating a child to lead a flourishing life, or making judgements about what a flourishing life will be for her, then I should feel equally uncomfortable forcing her to eat what I regard as healthy, or good, food, or to listen to what I believe is good music, or to read what I regard as enjoyable books. Or, for that matter, forcing her to attend a building for seven hours a day; to sit still and listen to what the teacher has to say; and forcing her to interact with numerous other coerced detainees with whom she may have no natural affinity. Once we have accepted the principle of parental obligation, we have accepted the paternalistic principle that we know better for the children what should happen to them than they do themselves. And, having accepted the principle, and the consequence that parents have the right to send their children to school, we have to ask to what purpose we should use the time they spend in the school. The simple answer is that we should use the time, at least in part, to facilitate their long-term prospects of living a successful and flourishing life.

How does this help us answer the questions? Well, we should not, as a general matter, presume that we know better than other people how they should best lead their lives. But becoming a teacher, a school administrator, or a parent, is adopting a role in which you have power over a child's life, and you know that the child is highly imperfectly informed about what will make for a flourishing life, and spectacularly ill-equipped to pursue one. If one is uncomfortable with the role, one should either avoid it, or carry it out despite one's discomfort.

Being more knowledgeable than, and having legitimate power over, a child, does not, however, give us a right to impose our particular view of how they will flourish on them. The paternalistic role is very complicated. We should not be guided by our own pre-existing views; rather, our views should be guided by our best judgements about the child and her interests — the kinds of things that will tend to her long-term flourishing. We can divide those interests into the general and the particular. Children have long-term general interests – interests that they all share, such as the interest in being able to secure shelter and food, and the interest in being able to make their own judgements about whether a particular religious way of life is a good one. But they also have particular interests, which are not shared, and which are much harder to identify. Norma may have musical talents which she has an interest in having cultivated, whereas Betty may be entirely unmusical, but have athletic talents through which she will flourish, if they are developed. Graham might be a very talented soccer player for whom soccer is a bore, and whose long-term flourishing will be better served by fostering his much lesser talent as an actor. Many parents will be familiar with the problem of a child who doesn't want to do her piano practice but who, the parents know, will benefit in the long run by doing the practice. But the parents also have the problem that some children *really never* get to enjoy playing the piano even if they do their practice and become proficient. Parents and teachers have to make fine-grained judgements about these matters with respect to particular children all the time. They make mistakes. But they at least have reason to be confident that, if they take their paternalistic responsibilities seriously, they are making fewer and less drastic mistakes than the children themselves would be making without guidance.

Policymakers and school administrators, by contrast, are not making fine-grained judgements about the particular interests of particular children. Rather, they must make judgements about the general interests of children, and how to set up an institutional framework within which those general interests are well served, and in which teachers – and, as they get older, the children themselves – can make and implement good fine-grained judgements about particular interests. The previous two chapters have argued for two general interests that we can understand all children to have, simply from knowing that they are growing up in our society, regardless of what else we know about them. In the first part of this chapter I am going to sketch out some of the general knowledge we have about the ways that modern conditions limit how well people can live flourishing lives. Then I shall argue that this knowledge has certain implications for the school curriculum, for what the school should offer as extra-curricular activities, and for the character of the school ethos.

We have a good deal of evidence about what makes people happy, and what does not make them happy. We also know that children have certain tendencies that make it very difficult for their families, even if they are well-intentioned and good judges of their children's interests, fully to prepare them for a flourishing life. Finally, we know that in our society there are certain quite specific barriers to living a happy and flourishing life which many of our children will have to negotiate, and that we cannot anticipate accurately which children will encounter, or be particularly vulnerable to, which barriers.

Richard Layard enumerates the central factors influencing our levels of happiness as the 'Big Seven': financial situation, family relationships, work, community and friends, health, personal freedom, and personal values.[1] We know that people are made happy neither by materialism nor by the wealth that materialism brings. Poverty makes people unhappy, and restricts considerably their ability to flourish, even when poverty is conceived as a relative rather than as an absolute concept. The low status and stress that accompany relative poverty, and the lack of control over one's conditions of life, diminish people's ability to flourish. But once people have achieved a reasonable level of financial security, additional income and wealth do not make them happier, especially if premised on the need to spend more hours at work and away from family and friends.

The income from remunerated labour helps people to have more control over their lives, and more security, up to a point, but it does not help much beyond a certain point. (As we saw in Chapter Two, this gives us good reason to be sceptical of the drive towards ever greater economic growth which politicians frequently advocate). We also know that people are happier when they are connected in social networks. Close connections to, and successful relations with, family and friends correlate closely with reports of subjective wellbeing. Being able to spend time with, and relate intimately to, other people is a tremendously important precondition of flourishing for most of us. Another important source of flourishing is the exercise of skills that are difficult to master. Those people who are lucky enough to have interesting jobs that suit their personalities and talents derive a great deal of flourishing from the exercise of those talents. But it is also common for people to enjoy activities in which they do not, by any absolute criteria, excel, but which make the appropriate demands on them; sometimes at work, and frequently outside of their jobs. Someone may find writing doggerel a challenge and find great satisfaction in producing ditties that just make his children, or his friends, laugh. Someone else might enjoy playing cricket as well as he can in a weekend team, not just for the companionship, but also for the sense of stretching his limited capacities. For many people, as I pointed out in Chapter Two, although it is important for them to be employed, or at least not to be involuntarily unemployed, it is in their leisure time that they will find the meaning in their life.

The evidence I have drawn on concerns *happiness*; it tells us within broad outlines what factors contribute to people leading happy rather than unhappy lives. Happiness and flourishing are not, however, identical. We often think of someone as flourishing when they achieve a great deal of value, even if we do not think that they are, personally, happy. An artist might be thought of as flourishing if she succeeds in producing great art, despite unhappiness in her personal life; indeed, we might still hold this view even if we think that the unhappiness itself produces the greatness. Conversely, if we believe that someone's happiness is simply the result of artificial stimulants, or is conditioned on ignorance about what is really happening around them, we do not usually think of them as flourishing. Consider, for example, someone who is happy only because she does not know that her 'friends' secretly despise her. Flourishing is a richer property than happiness, sensitive to many more features of a person's life than just her inner states. Any theory of flourishing is, furthermore, inevitably controversial: some readers will disagree with me that happiness and flourishing are not the same thing, while others will think of flourishing in a variety of religious terms, and others still in terms of the exercise of particular capacities or virtues.

How much of a problem is this? We have no direct evidence concerning what makes people flourish, both because flourishing is controversial, and because for any particular (controversial) theory, it will be hard to observe the causes of flourishing directly. It is interesting that Layard's 'Big Seven' factors in happiness correspond closely to elements in numerous religious and philosophical accounts of flourishing. They also allow for a great deal of diversity in the ways that people achieve happiness: acknowledging that people achieve flourishing through their engagement in friendship and family life, for example, leaves open numerous kinds of friendship and forms of family. I think, therefore, that it is fair to assume that the evidence of what makes people happy in the real world is also evidence about what makes them flourish.[2]

How can the evidence about what makes people happy guide education? Now consider the sort of challenges that children, as they grow into adults, will face in engaging with the world in a way that facilitates their flourishing. First, we know that family life is increasingly complicated by at least two factors. The first is that close to 50 per cent of marriages end in divorce, and a very high proportion of those divorces occur while children are still in the home. This means that most children who themselves marry will be in a relationship in which one partner has parents who are not married to one another. Furthermore, most divorced parents remarry, or re-enter a marriage-like relationship. So, as adults managing their own lives, they will have to engage with at least three, rather than the previously normal two, parental households. The time, energy, and emotional demands on a remarried parent are greater than those on an undivorced parent; the child of a remarried parent is not only negotiating with more households, but has to face more competition for the attention and interest of her parent.[3] Second, the dramatically increased geographic mobility in our societies weakens the connections among adults within families. Parents, adult children, and adult siblings, are less ready sources of mutual support and care when they live at great geographic distances from one another. In this way, even intact families are frequently less connected to one another in adulthood than was an expectation some 30 years ago.

A second striking phenomenon is the increased power of commercial influences over the public culture of our society, and in particular over children. Television has become a pervasive influence, and television content in the US is almost entirely driven by commercial imperatives. In the US marketers spent approximately $15 billion on trying to reach children alone in 2004.[4] In the United Kingdom commercialism is less pervasive, but still incredibly powerful, especially since the rise of cable and satellite provision, so that the public service broadcast networks are under heavy pressure to compete for audiences with commercial channels. The striking feature of commercialism in culture is that not only are the values that commercial interests promote not good values, but also the people promoting them do not believe them to be good. Consider Juliet Schor's encounter with the marketing industry:

> Children are being exposed to plenty of glamour, fashion, style, irony, and popular music, that is, sex. Even the family-friendly Disney Channel is full of sexually suggestive outfits and dancing. One Radio Disney employee explained to me that the company keeps a careful watch on the lyrics, but is hands-off with the other stuff . . . Emma Gilding of Ogilvy and Mather recounted an experience she had during an in-home videotaping. The little girl was doing a Britney Spears imitation, with flirting and sexual grinding. Asked by Gilding what she wanted to be when she grew up, the 3 year old answered, 'a sexy shirt girl'. . . . Mary Prescott [an industry professional] who is more deeply immersed [than other interviewees] in the world of tweening, confessed that 'I am doing the most horrible thing in the world. We are targeting kids too young with too many inappropriate things . . . It's not worth the almighty buck.'[5]

The mark of a marketing strategy's success is that it sells a product. Contrast this with the political, religious, and intellectual movements that shaped the public cultures of the Reformation, the Enlightenment, and the Victorian age. Proponents of values generally believed that the values they propounded were good, not only for themselves but for others. Of course, in many cases, they were wrong, and no doubt hypocrisy was not uncommon. But the cultural environment most of us inhabit now is one in which the most powerful forces attempting to shape the culture are driven by the desire to make large profits. In the United States, in particular, the spaces that are commercial-free are increasingly those that are largely uninhabited. It is hard to attend a public event, and almost impossible to attend a charitable event, which is not plastered in commercial, profit-seeking messages. These messages are designed, always, to target the acquisitiveness latent in most of us. And yet there is ample evidence that many of the things we acquire do not make us happy, or help us flourish, and also that fostering our acquisitive traits makes us unhappy.[6]

The third feature I wish to draw attention to is the financial complexity of modern life. Part of this consists in the relatively new phenomenon that people expect to live much longer beyond their working years than they used to, and do not expect to be supported beyond their working years by their children. Modern public health measures (including improvements in health and safety at work) and modern medicine have dramatically increased life expectancy for both men and women. Furthermore, the decreased connectedness of families and increased costs of childrearing have made children an ever less reliable source of support in old age. So, given the unavoidable political uncertainty attached to public pension provision (Social Security in the US), and its paucity, adults are faced with the relatively new task of saving adequately for retirement. Part of the challenge, though, consists in the flood of individual credit, provided not by merchants motivated by enlightened self-interest and imbued with local knowledge, but by finance companies motivated by profit, and almost devoid of local knowledge. Credit card companies have a powerful incentive to entice non-clients to become clients and to entice existing clients to enter long-term debt. Debt management has become a vital skill for individuals to have in advanced capitalist economies.

But the increase in leisure time as a fraction of one's life also presents a challenge and opportunity: what to do with that leisure time? There are more, and less, rewarding ways of spending one's leisure time. In a recent study of people's conceptions of freedom in the United States, the well-known sociologist Orlando Patterson found that a large percentage of women immediately thought of shopping as the time when they feel most free (men, by contrast, thought of driving).[7] But there is a good deal of evidence that shopping is not a very rewarding activity. Shoppers get a short-lived and immediate high from purchasing a new item, but that high dissipates rapidly.[8] For most of us, shopping for consumer goods is not something that conduces to our overall well-being. And because it is expensive, those who engage in a great deal of it must do more paid work. Activities that involve a person in developing and exercising complex skills and in engaging in intimate ways with others are much more likely to enhance their wellbeing in both the short and the long term. The economist Juliet Schor has even found that for teenagers, engagement in commercial materialist culture makes a significant causal contribution to various harms, such as anxiety, depression, and worsened relationships with their parents.[9]

I have made several comments about what kinds of activity tend towards flourishing. I do not regard them as particularly controversial, but I do understand that some readers will dispute them. Furthermore, many readers who agree with them will be uneasy at the paternalism involved in imposing these kinds of activities on others. It does not follow from the fact that I know better for Kenneth what would make him flourish than he does that I have a right to impose that flourishing on him. But, as I look at the implications of the comments in this first section of the chapter for what schools should do, bear in mind that I am not, in fact, arguing that children should be forced to live their lives in some particular way. Schools have a paternalistic duty to provide children with plentiful opportunities to develop the resources needed for living a flourishing life, and in order to do this, they have to deploy reliable information about human flourishing. But in doing so, they are not forcing a way of life on those children. The children will be subject to a myriad of other influences, and will, if their autonomy is facilitated as I recommend in Chapter One, be able to make judgements about how to live from among the alternatives realistically made available.

What can and should the education system do in response to the above observations, in pursuit of its obligation to prepare children to live flourishing lives?

Think first about the academic, or school day, curriculum. One mistake would be to divide it up into the 'vocational' on the one hand, and the 'life-preparing' on the other. We have the traditional academic curriculum – English, mathematics, languages, science, etc. – and this prepares children for success in the labour market. Then we have subjects like personal health and social education, alcohol and drug programs, parenting, religious education, social studies – and these subjects prepare children for life. And, perhaps, there are some subjects like art, music, cooking and physical education, which are in a grey area.

Why is it a mistake to conceive of the curriculum as divided up in this way? Mainly because many of the traditional academic subjects themselves present opportunities that are relevant to the child's long-term flourishing and are not merely preparation for the world of work. Some children come to a lifelong love of Jane Austen or Shakespeare or Rimbaud outside the school gates, but most of us who develop those enthusiasms do so only because we have studied these (or similar) authors in a classroom environment in which we have been manipulated or straightforwardly coerced to put in the effort it takes to read and appreciate their work. Children who are raised in a monolingual home within a society where their home language predominates will not usually learn a second or third language unless they are forced to by some agency – and, again, usually it will be the school. Some children will love the language they learn and some will deploy it in their paid work; but for many more it will be the gateway to learning about and engaging with a culture other than that of their society or subculture. More technical subjects such as mathematics and the sciences are perhaps even more rarely encountered outside the school in ways that facilitate lasting enthusiasm. But for some children, an enthusiasm for some aspect of mathematics, physics, or biology infuses their lives just as much as an enthusiasm for literature or music infects the lives of others.

This is the insight that underlies many traditional defences of the standard academic curriculum as a 'liberal education'.

The idea is that children have an interest, entirely independent of whatever interest they have in being equipped with job-related skills, in being acquainted with the greatest cultural goods that our civilization has produced. That interest derives from the fact that those goods can be goods for them, in the way they live their lives; the good constitutes what is sometimes referred to as the intrinsic value of education. In traditional conservative defences, the focus is often very much on literature and the arts, and specifically on Western culture. Both focuses today seem somewhat quaint. Non-Western societies have produced great cultural goods, and there would be every reason to acquaint Western children with some of those goods even if Western societies were not now, as they are, populated in significant part by people who see their cultural roots as belonging to non-Western societies. The case for cultural diversity in education does not depend on the idea that our society is diverse; it is only strengthened by that fact. Mathematics and the sciences are also great cultural achievements, and there are good 'life'-related reasons for including them in the curriculum.

However, it would also be wrong to try to fit *all* the demands of preparing a child for a flourishing life into the traditional academic curriculum. The observations I have made in the first section suggest four distinct kinds of educational experience that children should have, apart from the traditional academic curriculum. First, they should have classes in which they learn about family life, including good parenting and emotional development. Second, they should learn about what is sometimes called 'work/life balance', and how people deal with the demands of the workplace. Third, they should learn simple facts abut how credit markets work, investing and saving, and their obligations as taxpayers. Finally, they should learn something about what makes for a flourishing life, of the place of consumption and expenditure in that, and about how to use leisure time fruitfully.

Should these things be taught in separate 'subject' lessons? I don't have a view about this. The important guiding principle is that these issues must be engaged with in school in such a way that makes clear their importance for the children. Given the pressures on the time of teachers and administrators, teaching a subject 'across the curriculum' often, but not always, amounts to downgrading it, and sometimes amounts to not teaching it at all.[10] It is also important to teach in a way that does not confuse children into thinking, for example, that the main point of learning mathematics is so that they can balance their cheque books and deal confidently with credit card companies. These are valuable life-skills in our society, which schools are bound to impart, but they are not the main, or even a particularly significant, part of learning mathematics. I don't have the expertise to recommend a particular way of integrating the teaching of life-skills into the curriculum. Managers have to consider the circumstances of their particular school and school population, and integrate the subjects into the curriculum in the way that appropriately communicates their importance to the children.

Before commenting on extra-curricular activities and ethos-related considerations, I want to address two very obvious worries about incorporating life-skills issues into the formal curriculum. The first is that teachers will inappropriately bring their own biases and experiences into the classroom. In some subjects – cooking, for example – this is not a major concern. However, in others – such as when the issues being taught about concern marriage and family life, sex education, alcohol and drug-related education – this concern might be quite serious. The only sensible response to this concern is to admit that it is impossible to ensure that teachers will always succeed in treating their own biases with appropriate scepticism and distance. But this concern is no more weighty in this arena than in English, or in religious education or social studies. In Chapter Seven, I shall make some comments about how teacher education programmes and school managers could help to address the problem of teacher bias in educating children to be just citizens, and I think those comments are also applicable here.

The second concern about life-skills teaching is that sometimes they simply should not be taught in schools, because teaching them is either wasteful or counterproductive. Non-American readers will find what I am about to say incredible, but successful participation in a Driver's Education course is required for high school graduation in some parts of the United States. In most States it is legal for 16 year olds to qualify as drivers and drive a car on their own. Consequently, when Driver's Education is provided at a school, it is often taken by children aged 15 or 16, who start driving when they pass the course. Driver's Education courses, therefore, although they do not produce safer drivers, do encourage children to drive earlier, thereby causing a higher mortality and accident rate not only for those children but also for those who share the road with them.[11] Not only is the state spending money that could otherwise have been devoted to music, mathematics, or tax relief, but it is making the roads more dangerous in the process. The social science on alcohol and drug-related programs is less conclusively negative, but it is clear that numerous alcohol and drug-related curriculums are adopted without any evidence that they reduce the levels of alcohol and drug use or dependency which is, presumably, the only point in offering them.

I want to make two comments about this concern. First, where a curricular offering has a very clear short- to medium-term, and measurable, goal, then school authorities should be aggressive about ensuring that independent researchers rigorously evaluate the effects of the programme. On the evidence we have, all the States in the US should have a minimum driving age of 17 or 18 rather than 16, and Driver's Education as a curriculum subject should be eliminated everywhere at once. As with any curriculum offering, when it is relatively easy to acquire evidence about whether it meets its goals, that evidence should be gathered and acted upon.

But for most aspects of the school curriculum, whether labour-market or flourishing oriented, it is not at all easy to find out to what extent the goals are being achieved or what alternatives would be better. What is the goal, for example, of education related to the family and parenting? The main goal is to enable children better to negotiate the complexities they will encounter as they proceed through adulthood, so that they can flourish better in their personal lives and treat others with respect and humanity. How to measure success in this goal? And, unlike teaching children how to drive, it is inevitable that some of what goes on in school will relate to these matters, whether it is part of the formal curriculum or not. It would be impossible, for example, to teach literature without serious discussion of these issues, and it would be hard to teach history well without at least raising them. So formalizing the presence of the subjects in the curriculum, and ensuring that teachers and managers have reflected on what should be taught, what their goals are, and whether there is at least a plausible match between what is done and what the goals are, seems desirable.

The formal curriculum is only the main part of what goes on in a school. All schools have extra-curricular activities. Given that we force children to attend school for a very substantial part of their waking lives, we have an obligation to make school a congenial environment, in which they can, among other things, enjoy themselves in the moment. A substantial part of the motivation for providing extra-curricular activities should be to enable children to enjoy themselves. But school managers also recognize that for many children, extra-curricular activities present opportunities to encounter, sample, and make judgements about activities that they otherwise would never learn much about. Most of the children in the Latin club probably participate in it because they enjoy Latin. But many of the children who act or sing in the school play or choir, or who participate in the 16th Century Music Group, Free Tibet Club, or Young Gardeners Club probably participate initially out of curiosity, or are infected by the enthusiasm of a teacher or a friend. At least as much as the formal curriculum, the experiences in the extra-curriculum can give rise to lasting enthusiasms and long-term goals.[12]

Is there a rule of thumb for what kinds of extra-curricular activities to make available in a school? Obviously, the expertise and enthusiasm of the teachers will be a substantial consideration, and rightly so: it is hard for someone overseeing an activity to present it meaningfully to participants if that person does not believe it, fundamentally, to be worthwhile. But three considerations are worth bearing in mind. The first is that children vary enormously in their basic constitutions and in the kinds of activity they find to be rewarding. Second, numerous activities are readily available outside the school. So when the school replicates those activities, it is at best wasting an opportunity to broaden the perspective of some of its students, and at worst reinforcing the impression that those activities are the only ones available. The third consideration is that sometimes the school is the only location for a particular opportunity only because the school adopts that role. For example, it is quite unlikely that if US high schools withdrew from organizing American football, that activity would be unavailable outside the school. Whereas it is highly likely that if they refrained from offering a Latin club, that would not be available elsewhere.

The final consideration concerns the ethos of the school. I've talked a little about school ethos in Chapter One, and will say more on this in the second part of the book. But it is worth noting here how the ethos can affect not only how smoothly the school works from day to day, but also how children interpret their experience in the school. The ethos, in turn, is influenced by the interaction between a combination of factors, including the self-conception and diversity of the teachers; the composition of the student body; the school mission statement; the curriculum and extra-curriculum; the physical appearance of the school; the choices managers make about what kinds of activities to single out for praise and illumination; etc. So school leaderships in US high schools, for example, will often decide to shorten an academic school day in order to facilitate, or in some cases force, the whole school to attend a pep-rally for the football team; thus giving special endorsement to the activities involved.

Teachers adopt teaching personas, and in that capacity they will make decisions about how much of their interest in and awareness of commercial popular culture to reveal to the children; and also, how many and which of their own non-mainstream interests to reveal, and how. A school ethos that strongly identifies with mainstream popular culture and, for example, places special emphasis on prowess in mainstream professional sports, thereby tilts the experience of the children towards the interests that they would be likely to encounter and become enthusiastic about outside the school anyway. But a school with an ethos that is not exactly countercultural, but perhaps extra-popular-cultural, would deliberately valorize numerous different kinds of activity not readily promoted outside the school, on the principle that in doing so it would be widening the array of realistic opportunities for leisure-enhancing pursuits for children.

Even something as simple as the length of meal breaks and the kinds of meals available for children comprise part of the ethos of a school. The shift over the past 20 years towards lunches consisting of junk food represents an ethos change. The cafeteria-style lunchtime has replaced the sit-down lunch, and this evinces a different attitude towards eating and socializing, as well as encouraging self-segregation among the children. The length of time allowed for lunch is also relevant; a school that allows just 20 minutes for lunch (which is not uncommon in American public schools) encourages a certain attitude towards food, discouraging the idea that meals constitute an opportunity for relaxation and socialization. Some of these changes may be positive; the point is to notice that what may seem like fairly trivial and 'administrative' decisions about the life of the school do contribute to the ethos of the school which, in turn, affects its ability to fulfil its mission.

Schools, then, should see it as their task to facilitate their students' future and present flourishing. This, in fact, is the principle that lies behind the imperative described in Chapters

One and Two to facilitate their autonomy and prepare them for participation in economic life. In the next chapter I shall explain the final principle, which calls upon schools to foster skills and traits that will contribute not only to the individual flourishing of the student, but also, through their participation in political life, to the flourishing of others.

Four

I have focused so far on educational aims in which the benefit to the person receiving the education is foremost. In this chapter I want to focus on an aim that is usually justified by its benefit to other people. The child who becomes a well-functioning citizen in a democratic society may or may not gain from being so; but her fellow citizens benefit considerably, at least if she is accompanied by a critical mass of well-functioning citizens. If the children of today become the good citizens of tomorrow, they will commit less crime, be less rude, and contribute more carefully thought-out political input than if they become bad citizens; and everyone else will benefit from that.

However, the gain does not accrue *exclusively* to others. Most of us gain, too, from being good citizens. We exercise our powers of self-control, of rational thought, and of altruistic concern by being good citizens, and we also earn the respect of others; these things are genuinely valuable to us as well as to them. The good citizen, furthermore, is not completely inattentive to her own interests. While in an entirely just society she would always participate as a kind of impartial deliberator, in actual societies that are characterized by some degree of injustice, many children will grow up to be victims of injustice. In this way their participation, while motivated by impartial considerations, will, if well-considered and effective, be to their own direct benefit.

Both academic and political discussions of education tend to take it for granted that one of the central aims of schooling is to produce good citizens. Indeed, in the United States, which was the first country to institutionalize universal publicly provided schooling, the central justification was producing a unified citizenry out of a nation of immigrants with diverse pre-existing identities and loyalties. But there is much less agreement about exactly what constitutes good citizenship, and how it should be reflected in schooling.

The limitations of this book justify focusing on a specific conception of citizenship, rather than a general conception. A general conception would explain at a very general level what constitutes good citizenship in any kind of society. It would offer a general account which covered citizenship both in somewhat unjust societies, like ours, in which citizens have realistic avenues for protecting themselves against the most serious injustices; and also in radically unjust societies, like Hitler's Germany and Stalin's Russia, in which citizens had no protection against the arbitrary power of the state. For example, whereas I think that good citizens in a liberal democratic society should have an overridable disposition to obey the law, it is possible that good citizens in Hitler's Germany would have had no such disposition, and would merely calculate, for each law, whether to obey it or not. Certainly, whereas I believe that no British citizen in my lifetime would have been justified in assassinating a British political leader, I believe that any German during Nazi rule might have been justified in assassinating leading Nazis if the consequences would have been sufficiently positive.

I propose a conception of good citizenship in a liberal

democracy which has three central components, all of them dispositional.

The first is a disposition to abide by the law. The good citizen in a society that has democratic institutions, the effective rule of law, and reasonable protection of individual freedom should be disposed to obey laws that are passed by the government, even when she disagrees with those laws, and even when she believes those laws are unjust. This disposition should be overridable, because lawbreaking is sometimes justified in pursuit of justice or other great goods. Examples of justified lawbreaking are easy to come by; clear rules which obviate the need for individual judgement are much harder to formulate. So, for example, it seems to me that much of the law-breaking engaged in by activists in the Civil Rights movement in the 1950s and 1960s was not only justified but morally admirable. Any view which says that Rosa Parks was unjustified in refusing to move to the back of the bus would be wrong. One could easily be justified in driving the wrong way down a one-way street, violating a red light when it is clearly safe, or stealing a car, when doing so was the only way to save the life of a dying person (for example, by getting her to a hospital in good time). But the disposition to abide by the law is important because the rule of law is an valuable good for all who live under it.

The second, and related, element is a disposition to engage in political participation through legal channels to achieve justice and in pursuit of certain of one's own interests that it is legitimate to pursue. The first part of this disposition is easy to explain; when one is aware of injustice, one has an obligation to contribute to eradicating it. Since injustices are numerous, one must make judgements about how to distribute one's efforts, and the good citizen makes a calculation based on the probability of ameliorating injustice for any given ounce of effort she puts in. But she also, when legal and political channels are available, will be disposed to use those, rather than to use illegal means. The second part is more complex. All citizens have self-interested interests, and whereas it is legitimate for them to pursue some through political channels, it is illegitimate for them to pursue others. So, for example, whereas it is legitimate for a parent of a disabled child to lobby the government to provide better special educational needs provision, largely motivated by the interest that it will benefit his child, it would not be legitimate for *Archer Daniel Midland* to lobby the government to maintain agricultural tariffs, motivated largely by the interest in increasing its own profitability.

The complexity comes in because sometimes, if a system is wrongly set up to encourage people to pursue interests that it should be illegitimate to pursue, that may make their pursuit, in fact, legitimate. So, for example, the US system of representative government and campaign financing assumes that business interests will use political lobbying to extract rents (unearned benefits). This means that, in some areas of the economy, a segment that refrains from lobbying will be cutting its own throat, because to remain economically competitive it has to compete politically with other segments. The various segments of the transport sector, for example, have to compete with one another for the huge subsidies the US Congress expects to provide. If Rail decided to disengage from that process, it would be unfairly even weaker relative to its much better subsidized competitors (the airline, automobile, and trucking industries).

This matters for individual citizens not only because they might be employees or agents of such companies, but also because the same phenomenon can occur at the level of individual behaviour. The classic case is, in fact, the case of private versus public schooling. In the UK, where about 7 per cent of children attend private schools, a substantial proportion of that percentage attend schools that are designed to ease their entry into an economic and social elite. There is a strong case to be made that prohibition of private schooling would be legitimate, would improve state schools, and would increase equality of opportunity by preventing the children of wealthy parents from benefiting from parental wealth in one specific and illegitimate way. Suppose that case is good. If so, private schools should be prohibited, in which case no-one would be justified in sending their children to them. But private schools are, unjustly, allowed to operate, to the detriment (according to the argument) of the state schools. In this environment, a parent who otherwise would be unjustified in sending her child to a private school might well be justified. For example, she might rightly believe that in the available state schools, her child would receive an inadequate educational experience, and that in a private school he would receive an adequate experience. If she also believed that, if private schools were abolished, the available state schools would, in fact, provide an adequate educational experience for her child, she still might well be justified in 'going private'. Indeed, if she had good reason to believe that in the state school her child's experience would be unacceptable – the sort of experience no-one should have and that no-one would have if private schools were abolished – then she might be *morally obliged* to go private. The point here is that in a somewhat unjust society, one might be entirely justified in doing what one would be entirely unjustified in doing in a fully just society, and that the dispositions good citizens have with respect to pursuing their private interests should be sensitive to that.[1]

The first two elements of good citizenship are relatively uncontroversial. But my third proposed element is much more controversial, both in political and academic debates. This is the disposition to engage in political participation in a spirit of respect and a willingness to engage in public reasoning. This idea has been made most famous among academics by the work of John Rawls; political theorists Amy Gutmann and Dennis Thompson describe it as the 'norm of reciprocity'. They give the following account:

> Any claim fails to respect reciprocity if it imposes a requirement on other citizens to adopt one's sectarian way of life as a condition of gaining access to the moral understanding that is essential to judging the validity of one's moral claims.[2]

Another way of thinking of the norm is by saying that when we engage in politics using public reasoning, we should not make claims and arguments that cannot be accepted by others unless they already hold fundamental moral commitments about which we expect reasonable people to disagree. So, for example, if I argued that abortion should be outlawed because all human life is sacred and that this fact is made available through divine revelation, I would be violating the injunction; because some people who are entirely reasonable lack access to divine revelation unless they adopt my worldview. By contrast, to the extent that I am able to give reasons well grounded in the values people with quite different moral understandings share, I am abiding by the norm. Similarly, someone who argues that capital punishment should be outlawed on the grounds that executing another human being involves a wrongful substitution of man's will or God's will, would be violating the norm. The idea is that when we specifically put our weight behind the coercive power of the state, we should try to refrain from depending on reasons that we know very well could only by accepted by other people if they completely changed their worldview, as long as their current worldview is one that a person could reasonably hold.

The norm of reciprocity is nested in a specific conception of state legitimacy. This is that when the state uses force against its citizens, it owes them a justification of its actions. Moreover, that justification has to be one that they can, at least if they are reasonable, understand and could, in principle, come to share by the free exercise of their own reason. Appeals to revelation, to the authority of purportedly sacred texts, to naked self-interest, and to personal and unreproducible experience, don't have this feature. When those kinds of reasons are deployed as justification of coercion, a wrong is done to the person being coerced. If you like, you can think of this as a version of the requirement for the 'consent of the governed'. Opponents of some law or policy have more reason to consent to it when it has been justified to them in terms that they could, in principle, come to share than if no effort has been made to engage their own values in the justification.

The norm of reciprocity faces two very strong objections, so I want to address them both here. Both objections depend on the observation that the norm requires people to distance themselves from some of their deepest beliefs about what gives meaning and value to their lives. Deeply religious, and especially evangelical, citizens are often taken to experience this requirement most demandingly, since they hold (reasonable) views which they believe that others would be *much* better off sharing. They also sometimes believe that some practices are sufficiently bad for those who engage in them that those people would be better off being prevented from engaging in them. But their reasons for holding these views are not easily made available for scrutiny by people who do not already share their religious faith. So, for example, some religious citizens believe, on the basis of scripture, that homosexual practices are deeply wrong, and deeply harmful to those who engage in them. If I do not share their attitude towards the authority of scripture, I cannot accept that as the basis for viewing homosexual practices as morally harmful. If they use that belief as the justification for laws forbidding homosexual practices, or restricting the social goods attached to marriage to heterosexual couples, they are thereby violating the norm of reciprocity.

So the two objections are as follows. First, it is wrong for people to refrain from deploying their most fundamental moral beliefs in justification of political measures. People should, as a matter of personal integrity, deploy all the resources at their disposal, including what they sincerely believe to be the truth. Second, although there would not in principle be anything wrong with people exercising restraint in political action, it is wrong to *ask* them to do so, because it is simply too demanding — most of us, most of the time, are unable as a matter of psychological fact to divide our 'personal' and our 'political' moralities in the way that the norm of reciprocity expects.

I don't think that either of these objections succeeds in defeating the norm. Let's take the first. It seems right that people should act in their personal lives on what they believe to be the truth about morality. But as soon as other people are objects of their concern, there are limits on the extent that they can deploy the truth. This is both because we are highly imperfectly informed about the details of other people's lives, so that it is very difficult for us to apply our moral values in ways that render good judgements, and also because respecting other people's status as moral agents requires that we give them space to make their own judgements about what is good and how to pursue it. When we see another adult acting in a way that we think will lead them, but only them, into harm, it is right to use moral suasion, and it can be right to judge them as wrongdoers and allow that action to influence our own behaviour towards them, but it is often not right even to manipulate them, let alone forcibly to prevent them from acting in that way. The norm of reciprocity extends this insight to the use of state power. But it does so moderately. Whereas in our personal lives we typically refrain entirely from coercing other generally competent adults for their own good, even if we can explain the reasons that they should act differently in terms that they readily accept, the norm of reciprocity allows political power to be used when those conditions are met. Respecting other people's moral agency places some constraints on the ways in which we justify coercing them, and those constraints include distancing ourselves somewhat from our personal worldviews.

The response to the first objection suggests a way of dealing with the second. In fact the norm is not too demanding, at least for most reasonable people, because they can understand readily that they do not have a claim over how others lead their lives. They can understand that they are bound by a requirement to respect other people's moral agency, and they can endeavour to engage appropriately in politics. This is not to say that they will always succeed. Not everyone always lives up to the ideals they give themselves. If they did, that would probably be a sign of the weakness of those ideals, rather than an excellence in their moral characters. But the claim that if the ideal is sufficiently demanding that most people will, on occasion, fail to live up to it is not, in my view, damning.

Although I reject these objections to the norm of reciprocity, the second can be very instructive. Critics of the norm often point to the evangelical Christian community in the United States as an example of a community for whom it is excessively demanding. As I shall make clear in Chapters Five and Seven, I don't find this obvious. Even if it were true, I don't think this is evidence that the norm is in *general* too demanding. But what is instructive about the objection is that how demanding the norm is for any given person will depend on a range of institutional factors. For example, if the sphere of public discourse about politics is structured to elicit reasonable engagement in terms of public reason, it will be easier for just about everybody to observe the norm than if it is designed just to facilitate politicians rallying the faithful. If 30-second TV commercials are the main mechanisms of political communication, reasonableness is less likely to reign, other things being equal, than if politicians are pressured to participate in extended debates with each other and with other interested parties. Similarly, a system in which journalists routinely defer to the claims of politicians they interview is less likely to facilitate public reasoning than one in which journalists are well informed and approach their interviewees as equals.

In a system that facilitates public unreasonableness, the manifest public unreasonableness of some constituencies is not good evidence that the norm of reciprocity is too demanding. Evangelical Christians in the US know that they cannot expect reciprocation if they modify their goals in the way that the norm of reciprocity requires. They also know that even if they attempt to cooperate and compromise with some secular liberals, other secular liberals can resort to litigation to undermine any compromise. And like all other political actors, they know that if legislation transgresses the Constitution, the unconstitutional elements will get thrown out eventually. In case my comments so far have seemed one-sidedly critical of Christians, I might add that the willingness of some organizations like Americans United for the Separation of Church and State, and People for the American Way to resort to the law to prevent, for example, high school athletes from praying during school games is similarly motivated and similarly manifests unreasonableness. The system creates incentives to make maximal and unreasonable demands, and so discourages the virtues of reasonableness.

How should schools facilitate children developing the traits of good citizenship? I shall look at this question in more detail in Chapter Seven. But I do want to mention here three issues that demand attention. First, it is worth emphasizing again that schools are limited in how much they can compensate for the failures of the political system and the political culture. A political system that rewards criminality or unreasonableness will make it hard for schools to encourage conformity to the law or willingness to be publicly reasonable. Even in a reasonably well-structured political system, it may be very difficult to inculcate an inclination to abide by the norms of public reason.

Second, the ethos and composition of schools might matter as much as the formal curriculum. It may be that, even without much formal education pertaining to good citizenship, people find it easier to be law-abiding if they have been expected to exert a good deal of self-discipline in the main non-family setting in which they have been reared. They may find it easier to understand and empathize with the thinking of others who come from different cultural, social, or ethnic backgrounds if they have spent a good deal of time socializing with such people in a controlled atmosphere as children and adolescents.

Finally, the position of the child in the school resembles in an interesting way the position of the citizen within the state. The school has a major impact on the shape of the child's life, at least while she is of school age, and usually to a considerable degree beyond. School is also compulsory; whichever school she is in, it is not because she chose it against a wide array of choices, but because someone else forced her to be there. The way that a school is run, and the way a child sees her place in it, may influence the traits developed. I am emphatically not suggesting that schools should be internally democratic; children are children, and it is appropriate for adults to exert a certain amount of paternalistic power over them. But it may well be important that the school be seen to be set up for the benefit of all who inhabit it. It might be important, for example, that teachers exhibit a certain level of collegiality and solidarity, and that they and principals treat non-teaching staff with respect, as well as treating children with similar dignity and respect.

Part Two
Controversial Policy Issues

Five

The US and UK are at almost opposite poles regarding the state's stance towards religious schooling. Religious schools are legal in both countries. But since the 1950s, American public schools have exclusively been secular schools, in which it is not permissible for the schools to promote religious belief of any kind, to sponsor prayer, or to teach about religious texts other than as historical or literary documents. Americans are often shocked to find that in the UK the state collaborates with religious organizations in running schools that it, the state, funds. In many parts of Britain most state-funded primary schools are church schools (either Church of England or Roman Catholic schools) and the vast majority are served by at least one C of E and at least one RC secondary school. Some cities have Jewish schools, and in recent years Hindu, Sikh, and Muslim state schools have opened.

At the same time, some 7 to 8 per cent of American children attend private religious schools, which are subject to extremely light regulation. Religious schools in America are free to teach religious doctrines to their pupils more or less unconstrained by the requirement to serve secular purposes. Such secular purposes might include facilitating the autonomy of the children by, for example, teaching them about a wide range of alternative perspectives and ensuring that they understand that they are not required to be believers. UK religious schools, whether public or private, are bound by the National Curriculum which specifies secular purposes in considerable detail.

In both countries there have been moves recently to increase state support for religious schools. The 2002 Education Act in Britain facilitated expansion of faith schools, especially in the secondary sector, and senior figures in both major political parties have consistently called for such expansion. The school choice and voucher movements in the US have had considerable success, and the government now pays directly for low-income children to attend religious schools in Milwaukee, DC, Cleveland, and throughout Florida.

In both countries these developments have been met with fierce opposition. The three central charges are that religious schools undermine personal autonomy, that they foster social division, and that they fail at the task of producing democratic citizens. Religious schools are supposed to undermine autonomy by indoctrinating children in the school's religion. This is especially serious in those cases where the religion of the school coincides with that of the child's home; which is normally the case, since in neither country are children assigned to religious schools against the parents' will. Even schools that take an ecumenical approach to religious education, and educate all children about each other's religious backgrounds, are bound to privilege the sponsoring religion: or else, what is the point of being a *religious* school? Religious schools foster social division by being intrinsically divisive, in that children from different religious backgrounds are less liable to mix in school. But they also, the charge goes, do a poor job of fostering the kind of public-mindedness that is essential for citizens to contribute their share to the maintenance of a just polity. They encourage children to identify in a sectarian fashion rather than with the larger collective of their fellow citizens.

Critics of religious schooling in the UK recommend adopting the US model of separation of church and state. So public philosopher A.C. Grayling says that

> Society should be blind to religion both in the sense that it lets people believe and behave as they wish provided they do no harm to others, and in the sense that it acts as if religions do not exist, with public affairs being secular in character. The US Constitution provides this, though the religious lobby is always trying to breach it – while George W. Bush's policy of granting public funds for 'faith-based initiatives' actually does so. To secularize society in Britain would mean that government funding for church schools and 'faith-based' organizations and activities would cease, as would religious programming in public broadcasting.[1]

Within the US, opponents of vouchers for religious schools also appeal to the separation of church and state. But they also, frequently, appeal to the integrity of the religious schools which, they say, would be compromised by the government regulation and intrusion that would inevitably follow funding (as it has done in the UK). Sandra Feldman, the head of the second biggest teaching union in the US, expresses the objection as follows:

> For religious schools, public scrutiny and accountability raise issues of religious freedom; the deep infusion of religion throughout their curriculum and lessons is essential to them, as is their freedom to require children to attend religious services. They don't want state interference in any of that. Yet,

accountability to the broader public must go along with public funding.[2]

If the charges were true – that religious schools set themselves against children's autonomy and tend to make them bad citizens – surely the government should indeed adopt the separationist stance and refuse to have anything to do with them? Given the emphasis I've placed in Part One of this book on secular conceptions of autonomy, reasonableness in public deliberation, and, above all, on flourishing, the reader (especially the by now rather irritated, religious believer) might expect my answer to be 'yes'. But it is, in fact, 'no', and this chapter is devoted to explaining why.

I do not assume at all that religious schools all set themselves against autonomy, or tend to create bad citizens (where good citizens are understood in the ideal terms set out in Chapter Four). Many do a fine job on both counts, and many do a better job than many non-religious 'public' schools. But disputing the charge is less interesting for my purposes than disputing its *decisiveness* in the debate at hand. In the first part of the book I elaborated and defended a series of principles that should guide schooling; the principles of autonomy and just citizenship among them. But these principles should not just guide schooling. They should guide overall policy towards the education of children which occurs in the public space. A society, therefore, should act to optimize the chances that children will become capable of autonomy and acting as good citizens. It should, in other words, approach the regulation and provision of schooling not with the aim that each school will maximally implement these principles, but with the aim that each child will enjoy the benefits the principles try to serve. Depending on the political, social, and cultural context, the principles may be better implemented by providing space, and even support, for religious schools.

The 'separation of church and state' is an unfortunate red herring in this debate. The first reason it is that it just doesn't seem to rule out public funding of religious schools; in fact, it doesn't even rule out public funding of *churches*. The relevant clause of the First Amendment of the United States Constitution states that 'Congress shall make no law respecting an establishment of religion'. Of course, what this actually means in the context of living law depends on how it is interpreted by five members of the US Supreme Court.[3] But the best way of understanding the principle is as aiming to ensure that the state does not establish, or in some other way deliberately favour, a particular religious viewpoint. The state is supposed to have secular, not religious, purposes, and it is supposed to pursue just these purposes. If these purposes are best pursued in cooperation with religious organizations, as long as the state is not unduly favouring those organizations, there is no breach of the principle. If the state funded only Roman Catholic schools, because it deemed that only those schools taught the true religion, that would, clearly, be a violation of the principle. But if it makes its funding of schools conditional only on the successful pursuit of some secular educational goals, which are compatible with several religious viewpoints, there is no breach. The Milwaukee voucher scheme, for example, funds schools without regard to their religious affiliation, as long as they abide by the (secularly justified) regulations of the scheme. Contrary to Grayling's suggestion, this does not violate the principle, and nor do other faith-based initiatives which consist solely in establishing partnerships with religious organizations for the promotion of secularly justified policy goals.

The second reason that church/state separation is a red herring is that it is not, itself, a fundamental matter of principle. Several deeper principles support it; one of which is the desirability of people being able to reason to, and act on, their own judgements concerning religious matters. Having interpreted separationism in an implausibly strict fashion, Feldman and Grayling call for its implementation even at the cost of the prospects of developing personal autonomy. Think for a moment about Sandra Feldman's comment. She highlights the interests religious schools have in avoiding public scrutiny and regulation. But, absent public scrutiny and regulation, some children who attend religious schools are less likely to become autonomous, because some of them will attend schools that inhibit their autonomy. Some secularists regard this as a sacrifice worth making for the sake of maintaining pure separation.

More children might be more likely to become autonomous and just citizens in a regime in which strict separationism is maintained. And the numbers matter. It is plausible to think that no policy will achieve blanket coverage, so that the capacities are developed in all children; so it is right to aim for a policy that provides good prospects for a large number of children. But I'm going to explain why a more relaxed policy which allows some state funding of religious schools might promote these values better than a policy of not funding them. Most of the rest of this chapter is devoted to explaining why.

Anthony Grayling talks in the passage I quoted about secularizing British society. His vision of secularization involves society 'being blind to religion . . . in the sense that it acts as if religions do not exist, with public affairs being secular in character'. I disagree with him about the sense in which society should be secularized. There is nothing undesirable about having religious perspectives on public matters expressed and discussed. What is undesirable is that these perspectives, and others, should be advanced and evaluated in a mean-spirited and sectarian fashion. A secular society would not be one in which religion was absent from the public sphere. It would be one in which religious cleavages did not coincide with cleavages in public debate, and in which religious and non-religious perspectives were advanced and evaluated in a spirit of mutual respect; as the norm of reciprocity advanced in Chapter Four recommends.

Contrary to Grayling's recommendation of the American model of secularization, many secular American visitors to the UK are struck by two features of the public culture. First is the open discussion and debate about religious matters. Some politicians are openly atheist while others appear to be genuine believers: few make ritualistic and insincere invocations of God and the Bible. Openly atheistic and avowedly religious public figures discuss religious matters as if they were matters of real significance. The second is the fact that on any given public issue, multiple religious and non-religious perspectives are found on all sides. The public reasonableness of religious believers is particularly striking, in contrast with the US, where although religion is treated by the public culture as a purely private matter, it is beyond the pale for a politician to declare his or her atheism. In the US the boundaries between religious and mainstream culture are sharply drawn, to the detriment of the inhabitants of both, and religious cleavages are far more politically pertinent than in the UK. While the state does largely refrain from giving direct support to religious organizations, the society as a whole is less secular than in Britain.

How is this observation relevant to debates about schooling? Here is a conjecture about the mechanisms that reinforce religious sectarianism in the US. In the US parents must choose between secular public schools and religious private schools. The state exercises minimal control over private schools, and private religious schools have two markets: the religious sectarians who would send their children there even if there were public faith schools available, and the religious moderates who would choose public faith schools if they were available. Think of the choices this way: public schools offer schooling without a spiritual dimension, and sectarian schools offer schooling without a secular dimension. Religious moderates seek schooling with a spiritual and a secular dimension, but often face a polarizing set of choices. When the choice is between the public and the sectarian school, some religious moderates will send their children to schools influenced by sectarians rather than by secularists.

Because the public schools do not accommodate religious parents, those parents are more inclined than they would otherwise be to defect to sectarian schools. Consider the 1987 Tennessee case of *Mozert v. Hawkins*.[4] The Mozert parents objected to a Hawkins County public schools primary level civic education program using textbooks in which boys were seen making toast for girls, in violation of what the parents regarded as God-given sex roles; which quoted Anne Frank's speculation (false, according to the parents) that unorthodox religious belief was better than no belief at all; and which made (neutral, not approving) mention of witches and magic. The school district refused the parents' request to exempt their children from the curriculum, and the courts ultimately found for the school district. Secularists declared victory.

But now consider the actual consequences of the case. First, worried that school authorities across the country would shy away from their now controversial textbooks, the Publishers removed the offending passages from subsequent editions. Second, the parents removed their children from the district to a self-run school which taught fundamentalist values and which only children of fundamentalists attended. This resulted in reduced contact between these children and the secular world that might influence them, and which they might, in turn, influence. I suspect that if the state acted as it does in Britain, by cooperating with, but heavily influencing, religious authorities in providing schools, then the market for sectarian schooling would erode. In this event sectarians, rather than being able to influence the children of moderates, would have their children subject to influence by the mainstream and the moderates.

Sectarian religious entrepreneurs in the US are able to present the state as an enemy of religion. Stories abound among evangelical and fundamentalist Christians of bibles being banned from the classroom; of prayer groups being harassed by school authorities; of ministers and religious parents being excluded from school Parent Teacher Organization activities. In every case I know of where these stories contain a grain of truth, the courts have ultimately found in favour of religious freedom as properly understood – that is (in these cases) they found against the school authorities. But the grain of truth is enough for sectarian entrepreneurs. Independent information is hard to come by and not scrupulously sought by the fundamentalist community. And the unreasonably strict understanding some secularists have of the implications of state/church separation contributes to the alienation of religious communities from the mainstream public culture, and hence to the pertinence of religious cleavage to public disagreement.

The conjecture is just this: that a system in which the state collaborates with faith organizations in the provision of schooling is more likely to produce autonomy-facilitating schools and an autonomy-facilitating culture, other things being equal, than a system in which the state refuses to collaborate with faith organizations, but allows them to run their own schools independently. This is only a conjecture; as I've indicated, I don't know how to prove or disprove it. However, opponents of support for faith schools should take it more seriously than they do.

Notice that several things are happening in the story as I have told it. Schooling is a site of dispute between deeply religious believers and separationists. The resistance of separationists to supporting schooling with a spiritual aspect ensures that parents who want that for their children have to seek it outside the public school system, where they are free from secular influences on schooling. Thus their identity as religious believers (and perhaps their alienation) is reinforced, rather than challenged. Religious entrepreneurs can forge political constituencies more easily, hence society becomes less, not more, secular. By contrast, in the British case, where they are accommodated within the state schooling system, schooling is a site of negotiation and engagement between the deeply religious and the non-religious. Through processes of joint governance of schools, they are able to forge a certain degree of mutual understanding, and a degree of mutual influence is bound to occur. The true religious *sectarians*, who seek schooling without a secular dimension might get that; but they will go outside the public system, and there will be no need for deeply religious moderates to join them.

I've already outlined the ways in which strict separationism enables religious entrepreneurs to foster a sense of alienation between evangelical and fundamentalist Christians and the public system of schooling – a task that would become much more difficult by a regime of public funding of religious schools. But whether my conjecture about the US case is true depends on the motivations of parents and the character of American public schools. If the vast majority of parents who send their children to religious schools are true sectarians, whose only priority is guaranteeing that their children will come to share their own religious views and outlook on the world, then making available public schooling with both a spiritual and a secular dimension will do no good. If public schools are already sites in which autonomy and deliberative character are facilitated, there may be a significant risk of compromising this character by encouraging public author-ities to cooperate with religious entities in running schools.

There is no reason to believe either of these things, though. In fact, my suspicion is that the very features of American public schools that secularists ought to be uncomfortable with may be what repel religious parents from them. The typical American urban or suburban public high school has little in common with the liberal ideal of the autonomy and citizenship-facilitating common school. It is a 2000-plus stu-dent institution, in which no individual knows every other individual; in which many children never have any teacher for more than one year of instruction; in which the prevailing values include pep rallies for school sports and a slavishly conformist loyalty to the school and neighbourhood.[5] These schools maintain a deafening silence about spiritual or anti-materialist values, take sides in the Cola wars, and accept as a given the prevalence of brand names and teen-marketing. Religious parents often, with justification, believe that their own beliefs are at best ignored, at worst actively worked against by the schools. Since September 11 2001, countless school districts have enforced a morning recitation of the pledge of allegiance, a ritualistic affirmation of patriotism as a quasi-religious commitment. The reasonable liberal parent might be less than enthused about any children, let alone their own, attending such schools. There are, of course, better alternatives in the public sector, but few school districts or school leaders show signs of being inclined or able to foster it.

I suspect that in the US many parents are drawn to private religious schools not by any interest in having their children indoctrinated, but by their horror at the experience of the shopping-mall high school, and, in fact, an unarticulated sense that the values of the peer group, tolerated by the school, threaten, rather than serve, their children's prospective autonomy. If they do, I feel considerable sympathy. But fundamentalist Christians have managed to develop a counter culture in the US which includes a whole parallel world of rock music, kids' videos, and teen magazines. Margaret Talbot describes the magazines available for teenagers: 'It has its own magazines for every demographic niche, including Hopscotch and Boy's Quest for kids 6–13, which promise "No teen themes, no boyfriends, girlfriends, makeup, fashion or violence and NO ADVERTISING" '. Religious parents fear that schools that do not incorporate strong moral values, and which treat spirituality as just another lifestyle option, one which may not even be presented to children by sincere believers, endanger their and other children's prospects for a balanced and satisfying life.

Here are two examples. The first is drawn from my own experience as a parent. Shortly after my elder daughter started attending the local elementary school, she brought home a free glossy magazine called *Sports Illustrated for Kids*. It consisted of 32 pages of full-colour pictures of contemporary American sporting heroes, with a little text on each page about how brave, hard-working, and admirable these characters were. The personality on the front cover, and to whom more space was devoted than any other, was Kobe Bryant, a basketball player who was at that time facing a very public indictment on a rape charge. His defence, before the case collapsed, was that the sexual intercourse, which took place in a hotel room with a woman he said he did not know, was consensual. This behaviour contradicted the very carefully crafted public image he had previously projected of himself as a faithful family man. His wife is, as I write, in the process of divorcing him. The anecdote is not supposed to reflect especially badly on Mr Bryant; I imagine that in his circles such behaviour is unremarkable. But the publishers of *Sports Illustrated for Kids*, and the teacher who gave the magazine to her students, are complicit in promoting a certain set of values – in particular celebrity worship – which no parent can feel pleased about having endorsed. I took the infraction to be the result of a teacher being given free materials and having insufficient time to scrutinize them. But I would understand a deeply religious parent whose response was a fear that the school was deliberately, or neglectfully, inculcating wrong moral values. In the charged atmosphere of the American culture wars, these fears may be interpreted as, and may even become, demands for permission to indoctrinate their children. A more flexible policy might calm the atmosphere and lead to less sectarian demands.

The second example is, thank goodness, not personal. According to the website of its owner, Primedia, Channel One is shown to 8 million teenage children daily in American public (state) schools. The schools in question receive free state-of-the-art television and video equipment in return for ensuring that all their students watch a daily 12-minute news broadcast. Channel One pays for the equipment – and makes a profit – by selling 2 minutes of that broadcast to advertisers. The news content is entirely respectable, relative to the prevailing norms of news broadcasting. But the advertisements are for junk food, clothing, teen-oriented movies and music, and other teen products. Salacious trailers for adult-themed films are not uncommon. And all scholarly studies of the effects of watching Channel One show that children forget the news content but retain the commercial information. Again, from my secular-left viewpoint it seems that most administrators who force children to watch advertisements are innocent of bad intentions; they misunderstand in a profound way the purpose of schooling, and mis-value the children under their watch, but they are not actively trying to promote materialistic and consumerist values.[6] I can see, though, why deeply religious parents already alienated from the mainstream culture and the life of the public school might interpret these actions differently. These examples merely scratch the surface of the ways in which many public schools are imbued with the materialist values of consumer culture.

The upshot is that it would be unwise for Britain to follow America's example. But one live issue in the UK is that the government has recently begun to fund Hindu, Sikh, and, most controversially, Muslim schools. A great deal of fire is directed against Muslim schools because Islam is a religion which is supposed to be markedly more sexist than mainstream British society, so that the schools can be expected to diminish the opportunities of female pupils. I think the underlying supposition is open to dispute, partly because it is based on a very unnuanced understanding of Islam, and partly because it takes an unwarrantedly optimistic view about Christianity and the mainstream culture. But there is no need to dispute the supposition in order to defend funding of some Muslim school. Even if the supposition is true, it simply does not follow that Muslim girls will receive a worse education if the state funds some Muslim schools than if it does not. Whether the girls receive a worse education will depend on which schools they *would have* attended if the state *had not* funded the Muslim schools, and on how the schools respond to being funded. If the girls would otherwise attend private Muslim schools which have no reason to negotiate with the mainstream culture and its educational expectations, they are no worse off in funded Muslim schools. And the state has equal responsibility for their wellbeing, regardless of where they are going to school. It, and its taxpayers, cannot say, 'We are implicated if we fund the schools but we're off the hook if we merely permit them'. The state does no less wrong when it neglects children than when it pays attention to them.

One of the big differences between state-funded religious schools in the UK and the religious schools in the Milwaukee voucher scheme is the degree of control they have over which students to admit. Here is a place where the US model is probably superior. Funded religious schools in the UK retain the right to prefer students who are being raised in the faith that sponsors the school; some even require certificates from the local vicar or priest to show that the parents are regular church-goers. In the Milwaukee scheme, by contrast, over-subscribed schools have to select voucher students by lottery; they can give no preference to co-religionists. UK religious schools would do better at facilitating autonomy and deliberative character if they, too, were prohibited from discriminating in favour of co-religionists.

How would this help with facilitating autonomy and democratic character? If religiously based schools could not select on the basis of the family religion of the child, such schools would have a more diverse student population. And since the main way that children can be expected to learn about the articulation of the ways of life recommended by other religions is by observing the lives of their peers, this will give more opportunity for children in faith schools to become autonomous. But a second reason is that it will also give more opportunity for children outside faith schools to become autonomous. Contrary to the much expressed fear that faith schools undermine the opportunities for autonomy of those children who attend them, I fear that they undermine the opportunity for autonomy of *those who do not*. Children from secular homes cannot become autonomous without an appreciation of what the religious life involves, and this is something that, as I am only too aware, their parents cannot give them. They need children from religious backgrounds to be in their schools and their classes, which is more likely if those children are not hived off into faith schools. If faith schools are not allowed to select on grounds of family faith, and some children from atheist families apply, then more religious students will attend secular schools. Similar considerations, I think, suggest that the funding policy might facilitate democratic character.

Does this measure violate the right of parents to send children to schools that reflect their religious commitments? It would if they had such a right, but they don't. Catholic parents may well feel that RC schools are 'theirs'. But in fact they are public resources the purpose of which is to contribute to a just public system of education. Suppose an atheist parent chooses to send her child to an RC school so that the child will have a proper understanding of one of the world's central religions, and an enhanced opportunity to become autonomous. It is hard to see what reason the state could have to allow a child whose parents simply want her to be a good Catholic to be preferred over that child.

I've suggested that the UK would be wrong to follow the US model of having the government provide only secular schools. What about the United States; should it try to emulate the model embodied in the UK school system (and also widely used in Continental Europe)? The argument of this chapter is that there is no principled reason that it should refrain from doing so, and that doing so might yield improvements in the overall cultural environment. But in practice it cannot, at least in the foreseeable future. The political forces that favour state support for religious schooling are fiercely opposed to the appropriate kinds of regulation. Moreover the political forces that would be well disposed to appropriate regulation fiercely oppose state support, holding views like those I've attributed to Anthony Grayling and Sandra Feldman. State-supported schools will in the foreseeable future be overwhelmingly secular. Nonetheless, if school authorities are animated by the values I've defended in Part One of this book, they would do well to attempt to interact more than they currently do with the private religious schools in their regions, and also to make overtures to deeply religious parents of the kind that they routinely and rightly make to African-American and Latino parents. In particular, a school that adopts the goals of facilitating autonomy and democratic citizenship would take steps to ensure that its student population was religiously mixed, and that its ethos encouraged real engagement between children of different backgrounds. So although I am not optimistic that America's school system will evolve into the more complex kind of system found in most of Europe, one advantage of devolved local control is that it allows individual schools and districts to develop a much more inclusive and multi-faith ethos.

The strategy I've suggested is this. We should, when thinking about whether to fund religious schools, try to work out what impact funding would have on the overall likelihood that children will become autonomous persons and good citizens. Even if religious schools systematically serve these goals for their students less well than non-religious schools do, it still might be the case that a system in which religious schools are funded fulfils these goals better than one in which they are not, because of the side-effects of funding (and non-funding). This is especially likely when most of the children in the religious schools would be in religious schools whether or not they were funded.

Six

In the last part of the twentieth century, reciting the Pledge of Allegiance in American schools was a bit like the 'daily act of worship' in English schools – fading into obscurity except in certain districts. But in the aftermath of the events of September 11 2001, there was a flurry of legislative activity at state and local levels, insisting that public schools should inculcate patriotism in their students. The requirement that children recite the Pledge of Allegiance at the start of every school day was adopted widely. At high school level it is also common to require a 'daily act of patriotic observance', which schools are entitled to interpret for themselves. One interpretation is requiring the pledge; others include having a patriotic poem read over the school-wide announcement system, and a daily playing of versions of the national anthem over the announcement system.

The Pledge itself has an interesting history. It was authored by a Christian Socialist, Francis Bellamy, in 1892, to celebrate the 400th anniversary of Columbus's arrival in America. His intention was for the children to recite it in schools, thereby creating the kind of national unity which Bellamy saw as the prerequisite of a socialist planned economy. It was only adopted by Congress in 1942, when America entered the Second World War. The words 'under God' were only introduced as late as 1954: a McCarthyite measure to distinguish America's democracy from Godless communism.

Reciting the Pledge of Allegiance cannot, in fact, be required. Schools must, by law, allow students to refrain from reciting the Pledge with their classmates. However, for younger children especially, this can be difficult, and doing so requires parental support and toleration from the teacher. Schools vary in how encouraging they are of children to seek exemption. Consider the likely difference in effect between the following announcements (both taken from actual schools):

> 'We are now going to say the Pledge of Allegiance. You may refrain. Now stand and recite the Pledge!'
> 'We are now going to recite the Pledge of Allegiance. America values liberty, and it is your Constitutional right to refrain from reciting this Pledge. Now, those of you who wish to recite the Pledge, please stand.'

Proponents of inculcating patriotism do not always stop at advocating formal recitations. In the early 1990s a national debate exploded over the standards that should be required for teaching history in public schools. A document authored by Gary Nash and other prominent historians and commissioned by the National Endowment for the Humanities (NEH) advocated a new set of history standards. This was criticized, however, by Lynne Cheney, the Republican Chair of the NEH, for being insufficiently attentive to the activities of great Americans:

> Counting how many times different subjects are mentioned in the document yields telling results. One of the most often mentioned subjects, with 19 references, is McCarthy and McCarthyism. The Ku Klux Klan gets its fair share, too, with

17. As for individuals, Harriet Tubman, an African-American who helped rescue slaves by way of the underground railroad, is mentioned six times. Two white males who were contemporaries of Tubman, Ulysses S. Grant and Robert E. Lee, get one and zero mentions, respectively. Alexander Graham Bell, Thomas Edison, Albert Einstein, Jonas Salk and the Wright brothers make no appearance at all.[1]

Underlying Cheney's criticism is the fear that the kind of history these standards recommend will fail to promote attachment to the nation; in fact, she is worried that it will do the reverse:

The authors tend to save their unqualified admiration for people, places and events that are politically correct. The first era, 'Three Worlds Meet (Beginnings to 1620),' covers societies in the Americas, Western Europe and West Africa that began to interact significantly after 1450. To understand West Africa, students are encouraged to 'analyze the achievements and grandeur of Mansa Musa's court, and the social customs and wealth of the kingdom of Mali.'

Such celebratory prose is rare when the document gets to American history itself. In the US context, the kind of wealth that Mansa Musa commanded is not considered a good thing. When the subject of John D. Rockefeller comes up, students are instructed to conduct a trial in which he is accused of 'knowingly and willfully participat[ing] in unethical and amoral business practices designed to undermine traditions of fair open competition for personal and private aggrandizement in direct violation of the common welfare.'[2]

Nash's considered response to the criticisms is interesting, and reveals that on the fundamental issue of teaching children to be patriotic, there is a great deal of consensus. He says:

> The argument is in fact between two visions of patriotic history. On one side are those who believe that young people will love and defend the United States if they see it as superior to other nations and regard its occasional falls from grace as short pauses or detours in the continuous flowering of freedom, capitalism and opportunity. . . . On the other side are historians who believe that amor patriae is nurtured by looking squarely at the past, warts and all. Only this clear-sightedness will obviate the cynicism that sugar-coated history produces when youngsters get older and recognize 'the lies my teacher told me'.[3]

And, in fact, if you look at widely used US history textbooks, you will find numerous instances where the authors appear to be promoting national sentiment rather than impartially presenting and analysing information. Uses of 'we', 'our', and cognates abound, identifying the reader and author with their, in many cases long dead, compatriots. So, in many books, do identifications of 'America' or 'the nation' as an intentional agent. So, finally, do moralizing commentaries on the motives and characters of individual agents in history. Here are some examples from a best-selling high school US history textbook (all emphases are mine):[4]

- Explaining the entry of the US into the First World War: 'Most Americans, including the President, were drawn by powerful unseen forces towards the British cause. *We* spoke the English language . . . *our* laws and customs were built on English foundations. *We* had fought the American revolution to preserve *our* rights as Englishmen' (p. 208).

- Concerning the development of the Red Scare: 'The mania of these times would last even after the war. The virus of witch-hunting and super-patriotism was not so easy to cure' (p. 221). And later, during McCarthyism: 'The morale in the government service sank to the lowest point in our history' (pp. 375–76). General Douglas MacArthur was 'a true American hero' but, in his dispute with Truman over Korea, 'more and more Americans came to see that Truman was talking sense' (p. 366).
- In the section on the civil rights movement, Rosa Parks is described as a 'tired black seamstress', while Martin Luther King was 'a natural leader, American to the core', and in response to segregation he was 'indignant and saddened but not angry. He was a thoughtful man and a Christian' (p. 379).

Different textbooks moralize in different ways, emphasize different virtues and faults. They may even disagree not only about the significance but the moral content of events. But there is a striking consensus that such commentary and identification with the nation's past is appropriate.

This standard practice is markedly in contrast with the way that British educators tend to think of their job. Nick Tate, former head of the Qualifications and Curriculum Authority, opines that during his time at the QCA, 'There was such a widespread association between national identity, patriotism, nationalism, xenophobia and racism that it was impossible to talk about the first two without being accused of all the rest.'[5]

History teachers were particularly prone to making this association:

> The main problem is that history teachers by and large have redefined their role as providing pupils with skills and

concepts rather than as giving them a narrative in which
to live their lives. The English Civil War, from this point of
view, becomes an exercise in deconstruction, an example
of competing interpretations, a lesson in handling
evidence – no longer primarily a key event in the nation's
story.

In a recent survey of the views of European history
teachers' associations, England was part of a small minority
that did not consider heritage important, did not want to pay
much attention to national heroes, and queried whether
national identity was even a legitimate concept in a diverse
society.[6]

Tim Collins, the Conservative Party spokesperson for Education, echoed Cheney when he recently called for history to be
a compulsory subject up until the age of 16: 'Nothing is more
important to the survival of the British nation than an understanding among its young of our shared heritage and the
nature of the struggles, foreign and domestic, which have
secured our freedoms.[7]' Who is right? Should we use schooling, and history teaching in particular, to promote patriotism?

The first puzzle to address is Tate's observation that several
concepts get confused. Xenophobia and racism are quite different from patriotism and a sense of national identity (I shall
avoid using the term 'nationalism' because its meaning is
much less well fixed than the others). But patriotism is susceptible of several interpretations. On some interpretations the
patriot owes special loyalties to his fellow countrymen; he
should put them first when deciding what to do in certain
situations. This might sound like racism or xenophobia, but it
is not. The obligation-patriot can perfectly well limit the situations in which we have to put our compatriots first to those

cases where the needs or interests of foreigners are not pressing, or where they are just not more urgent. Consider the analogy with the family; I have an obligation to help my daughter with her homework, but not to help the next-door neighbour's daughter with her homework. But if my next-door neighbour's child needs a blood transfusion to survive, and I am the only person with compatible blood, I am obliged to give blood, even if doing so will compromise my ability to help my daughter with her homework (because I'll be too tired).

A weaker sense of patriotism says that when our compatriots and foreigners are both in need, I am permitted, but not required, to put my compatriot first. According to this view, for example, we might say it is permissible, but not required, to make donations to domestic charities instead of overseas charities, when those charities make similar contributions to people's wellbeing. The patriot is the person who makes use of that permission.

But there is a weaker sense of patriotism, still, which I think meshes well with the concerns that Cheney and Tate raise. According to this view, the patriot is the person who feels a special sense of identification with his compatriots. He might also feel specially obliged to them, or specially permitted to put them first. Or he might not; he might simply feel an identification with and affection for his country and his compatriots, which does not give rise to any special obligations or permissions. Patriotism in this sense has no real connection with racism or xenophobia. It can be connected, indeed, with a sense of national shame or inferiority. For example, a Briton might feel a special sense of shame that Britain has failed to rid itself of the monarchy, or a particular embarrassment at the poor structure of Britain's welfare state relative to those of

Sweden and Denmark. What could be wrong with teaching patriotism even in this very weak sense?

Let's think first about why someone might want to promote patriotism in this sense. Neither Tate nor Cheney (nor her critics) is very explicit about this. They just seem to assume that a sense of identification with one's compatriots is a good thing, but don't explain why. Here, then, are several common reasons for seeking to promote patriotism:

1 **Obligation:** People do, in fact have special obligations to put their compatriots first, and they will be more likely to discharge these obligations if they are taught a sense of national identification.

2 **Solidarity:** Patriotic identification helps to underpin the sense of social solidarity we need to achieve in order for people to be willing to make the sacrifices necessary to achieve and maintain a just distribution of liberties, opportunities and resources in society.

3 **Citizenship:** People who have come to identify with their compatriots will find it easier to develop and exercise the traits of the good citizen. In particular, it will be easier for them to modify their demands with reason, if they acknowledge those they are arguing with as people with whom they identify.

4 **Flourishing:** Identification with a particular place and the people in it is an important component of human flourishing. Being connected to other people makes a vital contribution to most people's sense of wellbeing, and encouraging patriotic sentiment helps them to feel that sense of connection with the people in their immediate vicinity.

What should we make of these reasons? It is, in fact, very difficult to show that people have distinctive obligations to their fellow nationals, which override obligations that reach wider. The saying 'charity beings at home' makes (some) sense as an acknowledgement that we would be surprised to find someone who cannot act charitably to their nearest and dearest acting charitably to more distant others. However, it does not express a fundamental prescription, certainly if 'home' is understood as 'the country'. Why would countries, the shapes of which change over time in response to arbitrary actions like wars, invasions, and intermarriages, precisely describe communities of mutual obligation? This question is hard to answer, and it is harder still in a world of international social and economic institutions. For not only do national elites interact much more with members of other national elites than with many of their own compatriots, but market-mediated interactions occur all the time between individuals in different countries, and these interactions can be life-and-death matters for some of the parties. On top of that, the terms of trade themselves are mediated by intergovernmental agreements; Americans and Europeans exert power over individuals in developing countries not only when their armies invade, but also when their governments resist efforts to proscribe agricultural subsidies through the World Trade Organization. Our lives are profoundly interlinked with those of strangers, and for most of us in the rich world, our actions implicate some foreigners more than most compatriots.

It's worth looking at two kinds of argument in favour of countries as arenas of mutual obligation. The first draws on the analogy with the family I made earlier. Just as we have special obligations to our family members, so we have special obligations to our fellow countrymen. But this is not a good analogy. Family members maintain intimate relationships with one another which do, indeed, give rise to special obligations, especially between parents and children. Intimacy is simply not characteristic of relationships among fellow nationals; we do not even know most of our co-nationals, or have anything in common with them other than nationality. The second argument points out that, because we share a state with our fellow nationals, we are in a particularly strong position to render them vulnerable to our decisions; we can, in particular, command the state to exercise coercive power over them. So we are specially obliged to help them meet us as equals in the political domain. This argument has more power, but is spectacularly ill-suited to demonstrating special obligations among co-nationals in powerful nations. We are all too aware that citizens of poor nations in the world are at least as vulnerable as poor citizens in our own countries to our decisions about the use of state power. Even the poorest British and American citizens have institutions that protect them against the willingness of their wealthy co-nationals to do them harm through the use of state power. However, citizens of poor countries should be aware that they have no such protections.

Does patriotism help to establish the kind of solidarity that underpins people's willingness to make sacrifices for each other? Does it help citizens to modify their unreasonable demands against one another? It may do both of these things. The worry is this; co-nationals are not the only people we have to treat justly, and a policy of encouraging identification with co-nationals for the purposes of getting them to treat each other better may risk making it harder for them to treat foreigners justly as an unintended side-effect. There is a simple explanation for Tate's observation that history teachers often identify patriotism with racism and xenophobia, and that is that British patriotism has often, indeed, carried with it both racism and xenophobia. He is right that they are distinct phenomena, but it does not follow from their conceptual distinctness that promoting patriotism (which is, in principle, morally innocent) will not have the side-effect of causing xenophobia and racism (which are morally vile). Normally in British history the three phenomena have been closely associated, and this fact is what the history teachers are reacting to. German patriotism is similarly tainted by history, as is the patriotism of many other countries. Even in the US, which is unusually inclusive in its understanding of the 'nation', nationality is sometimes used (both by liberals and conservatives) in ad hominem point-scoring (Arnold Schwarzenegger's Austrian origins were used by some opponents to cast doubt on his suitability to serve as California Governor, for example).

Patriotism can, similarly, be used to interrupt the flow of free and rational political debate within a country. David Miller, a prominent defender of a moderate form of national-ism, evokes the more-or-less benign national sentiment that the British often pride themselves in when he quotes Kenneth Grahame's Water Rat from *Wind in the Willows*:

> Beyond the Wild Wood comes the Wild World. And that's something that doesn't matter, either to you or me. I've never been there, and I'm never going, nor you either if you've got any sense at all. Don't ever refer to it again, please.[8]

Contrast the Water Rat's words with Leon Rosselson's sar-donic lines:

> The state of the nation is all my concern
> When I'm gnawing a crust for my dinner

> I can't afford meat on the money I earn
> And I'm growing steadily thinner
> But it's all for the good of the nation.
>
> The nation, the nation, the nation is in such a terrible
>   state,
> Stagflation, inflation, if we all pull together we'll once
>   again make Britain Great.[9]

Promoting patriotism on solidarity and citizenship grounds is playing with fire, even if the national sentiment in play is relatively benign. It may cause people to neglect their duties to foreigners; this is the danger suggested by Ratty's comments. But it may also cause them wrongly to refrain from demanding justice for themselves (this is Rosselson's point) and even if it does help 'the right' people to modify their political demands against their fellow countrymen, it may encourage them to make *wrongful demands* against foreigners. This is a reasonable worry even when the country in question does not have a particularly objectionable record of internal injustice or of wrongdoing against other countries. When it does have such a record, promoters of patriotism should be particularly cautious. Patriotism in fact sometimes interferes with the process of reasonable debate by enabling some participants to call into question the good faith of their opponents. No-one doubts that it is possible for many people to be good citizens without being patriotic. However, if patriotism is prevalent, it will be possible for patriots to distort the way that other patriots receive the opinions and arguments of non-patriots. This will be especially problematic in times when the nation in question faces, or believes that it faces, some sort of external threat.

I think the best case for promoting patriotism in schools, in fact, is the flourishing argument. It seems right that a sense of identification with fellow countrymen, and with one's country more generally, helps many people to make sense of their environment, helps them integrate into it, and makes them feel good. I have a particularly complicated relationship with nationality; I am a British national who has lived most of my adult life in the United States, and I have a strong sense of identification with, and affection for, both countries. I notice, especially, the affinity I feel with Britons when I am in the US, and the affinity with Americans when I am in the UK, and my tendency to bristle at English anti-Americanism and the strangely condescending Anglophilia some Americans evince. This is a contribution, I think, to my welfare, and I see the same in others.

But national identification is only one source of flourishing: it is not essential in the way that I suspect identification with one's family is for most people. It is more like enthusiasm for a particular sport, or for a particular kind of music; it makes a real contribution to a person's sense of wellbeing, but if it were not there that person would substitute some other enthusiasm or locus of identity. If it were *essential*, there would be a strong case for promoting it, on the grounds that schooling should promote children's prospects for leading a flourishing life. But if it is just one of many valuable sources, the case is much weaker. The case is weakened even more by the observation that in most stable countries most of the time, the background culture will exert plenty of influence towards patriotism. Politicians and political organizations are liable to create their own pressures towards patriotic identification. Of course, popular culture is somewhat cosmopolitan, especially outside the United States (because outside the United States a great deal of the popular culture that is consumed emanates from within the United States) but even so most countries have indigenous popular cultures which seep into children's consciousness. On top of this there is probably a strong tendency in our natures to identify with our immediate surroundings when those surroundings are reasonably appealing and not unduly hostile. Patriotic identification is often a non-inculcated response to the lovableness of the country in question.

So I do not think there is a good case for teaching patriotism in schools, whether through skewing the curriculum towards love of country, or through more symbolic acts, such as organizing students to recite the Pledge of Allegiance or salute the flag, even when these activities are clearly voluntary.

So far, though, I have not presented a case *against* teaching patriotism in schools. We teach many things that there is no particular justification for teaching. What is especially bad about teaching patriotism? There are two reasons to be particularly reluctant to teach patriotism. The first invokes a principle I have not discussed before: the principle of legitimacy. The second concerns the educational distortions that I think are inevitable if we try to promote patriotism within a particular subject area.

The legitimacy problem is rather simple. We think it is very important for states to be just. But we also think it is important for them to be legitimate: for them to enjoy the consent of the governed. But it is not good enough simply to have consent; consent is legitimizing only to the extent that the agency being consented to has not manipulated the people into consenting. Imagine a parent who enjoyed the unreserved adoration of his daughter (normally a good thing) and then revealed that he got this adoration by systematic deceit and manipulation. The adoration is tainted by the process from which it arose. Similarly, the legitimacy argument goes, consent is tainted if the government itself produced it, not by winning it, but by manufacturing it. But the education system is an agent of the state; if we allow the state to use that system to produce sentiments in the populace which are designed to win consent for it, it thereby taints whatever consent it subsequently enjoys as being non-legitimizing. Something like this is precisely what is going on when British schools celebrate the monarchy (as did some that I attended), and when American schools organize children to cite the Pledge of Allegiance. Consent is being manufactured not won, and it therefore does not legitimize.

The second problem is the distortion problem. This has two dimensions. First we have good reason to worry that when the state uses its agency (the education system) to promote patriotism, it will wrongly influence the character of the vision of the country that children come to have. It is certainly the case that the legislators who imposed patriotic observances in American schools were not intending to promote careful and thoughtful give-and-take among students concerning what America is and what is good and bad in it. Rather, they were trying to promote their own, particularistic, vision of America, the one that is associated with compulsory patriotic observance. Patriotism gets its purchase from the fact that in a diverse country, people have different and competing visions of what is good about their country, and can learn from one another. Distorting this process of vision formation and re-formation is undesirable.

The second dimension of the distortion problem applies specifically to adopting the promotion of patriotism as an aim in the regular curriculum. Because it is the discipline most commonly targeted for patriotism promotion, I shall focus on history, but I suspect what I have to say will apply to other disciplines too. Think about the purposes we have when teaching history in schools. Here are three:

1 **Truth:** It is legitimate to try to establish and convey the historical truths; to teach what actually happened, in so far as we know that. It is legitimate to teach children that Europeans came to the Americas in the fifteenth century, that the British colonies rebelled late in the eighteenth century and established an independent federation of States; that Prince Metternich's diplomacy was motivated by the desire to delay the collapse of the old order in Europe for as long as possible, and that Henry Kissinger was a biographer of Metternich before becoming Secretary of State; that there were revolutions throughout Europe in 1848, that Henry VIII ultimately left the Roman Catholic church and established a church of England; etc.

2 **Causation:** It is legitimate to teach children how to go about discerning causal connections in social processes and, perhaps, more importantly, to teach them what difficulties are involved in discerning such connections. It is legitimate to teach them that there are disagreements about the causal processes which led to the invasion of England in 1066; about those leading to the First and Second World Wars, and the Civil War in the United States; about the fall of the Roman Empire and the rise of the English industrial working class. We should teach them what kinds of evidence count in favour and against causal hypotheses and, importantly, that the available evidence is often not completely determinate.

3 **Parochial history:** It is legitimate to focus particularly on the history of the institutions our children can be expected

to inhabit, so that they can more effectively and knowledgeably negotiate those institutions. In the American context, this would involve teaching about the development of the two-party system and the way that the parties have changed electoral laws over time; the evolution of the Constitution and changes in constitutional interpretation and the kind of reasoning that is accepted as legitimate in public debate and judicial review; the development of the New Deal and Great Society programmes and the paths not taken; the ways that political power has been sought by different movements and interest groups. It is legitimate both to teach this so that children can come to understand the institutions they will operate within, and to think critically about those institutions themselves; so that their endorsement or rejection of the institutions is reasoned and informed.

My conjecture is that the aim of inducing patriotic senti- ment will interfere with these legitimate purposes. I can't prove this, because to do so would require an exhaustive exploration of all methods of teaching history, for which I lack the space. But think about some particular cases. Take the first aim. A good deal of what actually happened makes any coun- try distinctly unlovable to someone possessed of an effective sense of justice. I suspect the conservative patriots in the US are right to want anti-communism, Hiroshima, Watergate, the secret war on Cambodia, and slavery to be glossed over rather quickly. The persistence of poverty in the midst of the American Dream and the lengths to which the state has gone at various times to inhibit the success of movements for social justice is quite impressive, and cannot reflect well on the nation itself. British imperialism, in its turn, is distinctly unlovable, and the manifest willingness of many working-class organizations in Britain to partake in the benefits of imperialism makes it hard to think of imperialism as incidental to the history of the 'true' nation. The truth is frequently inconvenient and may suffer in pursuit of patriotic sentiment.

Now consider the second aim. An educator who has anywhere in her mind the purposes of instilling love of country will have a hard time teaching about the causal processes which led up to the Civil War in the US, especially given the preconceptions her children are likely to have. I had a conversation with two colleagues about the different ways we were taught about the causes of the US Civil War. A white colleague from the South was taught the war was about protecting states' rights from the encroachments of an increasingly powerful federal government; a black colleague from the North was taught it was about preserving the union and abolishing slavery; I (in the UK) was taught it was about creating flexible labour markets and liberalizing trade. Only one of these explanations reflects well on the moral character of the war; while it is not the least plausible, it is not the most plausible, and the others all have some plausibility. The teacher concerned with imparting the ability to reflect rationally on causal connections must encourage reflection in the light of the best evidence she can present, and discourage that any of that reflection be distorted either by her desire or that of any of her students to present the events in a favourable light.

Patriotic concerns when teaching the Civil War are also likely to inhibit the third aim. The American Civil War was the first war in which whole societies were mobilized, resulting in a vast casualty count and economic devastation. Because it resulted in the emancipation of the slaves, and because the unjust effects of slavery persist into the present, it continues to have a central place in the moral story Americans tell themselves about their country. One cannot understand contemporary American political institutions without an accurate picture of the Civil War, yet teaching the complexity of motives of both sides (many of which were morally obnoxious, again on both sides) is unlikely to contribute to love of country.

After her first encounter with the history of the Civil Rights movement, my daughter (then aged 6) came home and told me about Rosa Parks. She repeated to me the myth, which she had been told, that Rosa Parks was a 'tired old black lady' who one day just decided that she would refuse to go to the back of the bus, thus sparking the modern movement for Civil Rights. We have seen above that this is repeated in Boorstin's text book (which is for secondary school students) and the American readers of this book almost certainly have been told this during their own schooldays, and some may believe it.[10] It is, strictly speaking, true that Parks was a black seamstress, though no-one who has deliberately decided to flout the law publicly can believe that she was tired. What is conveyed is that she just finally snapped, and thought something to the effect of 'I'm not going to take this any more'; and that her spontaneous refusal prompted a spontaneous protest movement.

This is a very convenient myth, and reflects a certain romantic, but factually inaccurate, view of the way that social changes occur. In fact, Parks was a political agitator who had trained at the famous Highlander School, which to this day plays an important role in training and developing radical activists. She was selected by the NAACP for the role she took on precisely because she had deep roots in the community and was widely respected. The organization believed that she would have the stamina and iron will needed to sustain a long fight, and the widespread support needed to win. Teaching about Rosa Parks in a way that perpetuates the patriotic myth of great people reluctantly coming into conflict with injustice must distort the way that children come to understand the political processes they themselves will eventually participate in, even when what is said is not, strictly speaking, false.

Patriotic sentiment is complex. It has good consequences, both for the person who experiences it and for others. It also has bad consequences. Teaching patriotism in schools runs a serious risk of violating the liberal principle of legitimacy of distorting and narrowing children's visions of the nation, and of interfering with schools' abilities to deliver on some of their pedagogical obligations. In sum, we should not do it.

Seven

Prior to 2002 in the UK there was no systematic, nationally coordinated effort to inculcate citizenship in children through schools. Many individual schools incorporated a concern with citizenship in their mission statements, ethos, and teaching practices. For example, it has long been common to teach religious toleration in religious education classes (RE being one of the few compulsory subjects in the 1944–88 system) and to use English and, to a lesser extent, history classes to teach children how to reason about moral and political matters. There's also an old tradition in English schools of using games (sports) as an arena for teaching the virtues of good citizenship; in particular, team work, leadership, and being good losers and magnanimous winners.

But in 2002 citizenship education became part of the compulsory National Curriculum for schools in England and Wales. It is a small part of the compulsory curriculum, and schools have a great deal of latitude in how they integrate it into the life of the school. The National Curriculum suggests that primary schools should aim to 'cover the knowledge, understanding and skills that prepare pupils to play an active role as citizens. This promotes pupils' personal and social development, including health and well-being.' Secondary schools should aim to:

reflect the need to ensure that pupils have a clear understanding of their roles, rights and responsibilities in relation to their local, national and international communities. The three strands in the programmes of study to be taught are:

- Knowledge and understanding about becoming an informed citizen;
- Developing skills of enquiry and communication; and
- Developing skills of participation and responsible action.

The United States has no similar national programme. But there are numerous private foundations devoted to promoting civic or citizenship education in schools, several States incorporate concern with promoting citizenship in their State Standards, and some schools incorporate it in their social studies curriculums. A fairly typical statement of intent comes from the Indiana Department of Public Instruction:

Citizenship education examines the conduct of the individual as part of a democratic society. External behaviors of 'good citizenship' are identified through participation in the larger society with those behaviors contributing to the 'common good'. Citizenship education begins at an early age as we emphasize the rules of good social behaviour as well as benefits to be gained from those actions. In school, citizenship education is developed through classroom participation, elections, decision-making opportunities, social action to benefit the community, and similar opportunities for students to feel a part of the larger community and that their contributions are valued. Good citizenship opportunities in the school can translate into greater community involvement as an adult with greater voter turnout, service on juries, and involvement in community endeavors for improvement.[1]

It is not clear to what extent schools and teachers actually incorporate these standards. As American schools are not inspected or evaluated in a rich way, and because most administrators are under multiple pressures, it is easy to imagine that it is not a high priority.

In Chapter Four I argued that schools should have, as one of their goals, equipping students with the skills, knowledge, and habits that tend towards good citizenship, where good citizenship is understood in a fairly demanding way. One apparent consequence of that might be that I should welcome the initiatives designed to promote citizenship education. But, as usual, things are a little more complicated.

Citizenship education was introduced in the UK without a great deal of opposition, and, as my comments about US educators in the previous chapter implied, it is popular across the political spectrum within the United States. So it is worth considering what has triggered the movement for citizenship education, before looking at some of the problems and pitfalls that schools face in promoting good citizenship.

Of course, arguments for mandating or encouraging citizenship education are various, but one central argument in both the US and the UK concerns declining levels of civic commitment from citizens. This declining commitment is inferred from two phenomena: (a) the long-run decline in voter turnout at elections and (b) the decline in what some political scientists call 'social capital' – the wealth a society derives from the regular and frequent social interactions between people in civil society, for example, participation in trades unions, churches, sports clubs, bowling leagues, parent–teacher associations, etc. The observation is that individuals are less engaged in their communities, as well as in the political life of their country, and that this has bad effects on political outcomes and society's ability to respond to the needs of its citizens.

The problem with this argument is that it is not really an argument for citizenship education in schools. If we think that young people are emerging from schools as incapable or bad citizens, that is a bad thing. But that is not the phenomenon being observed. We observe *low participation* in various important processes, the explanation for which might lie in the structure of those processes rather than in the citizens themselves.

We can think of the possible barriers to participation in civic and political life as falling into two categories, *viz.* material and subjective. What are the material explanations for the decline in participation? Technology has made possible, and the economy has made rational, new relationships between work and home. More people live further from work than before; they are therefore much less likely to live near their workmates, and so there is a greater cleavage between the networks of work and home life. People move jobs and homes, more often than they used to, so that their friendship ties with their neighbours and workmates are shallower and harder to develop. They live further from their extended families, which raises the costs of childcare (and therefore of participation in civic and political activity). They work longer hours, leaving less time available for leisure and participation. Changes in the status of women has made them more reluctant to subsidize men's involvement in public affairs by carrying the entire burden of childrearing and housekeeping: it has also made both them and the men to whom they are married more eager to spend time together. Each of these changes (some bad, others good) constitutes a material factor in the decline in participation, but citizenship education will do little, if anything, to address them. In so far as the material barriers to participation explain the decline, there is no reason to believe that improving the education of citizens will improve participation, because it doesn't address the systemic factors. So citizenship education is not a panacea for either the moral malaise in contemporary capitalist societies, or the declining levels of participation in the political process and civil society.

But if we turn to the subjective explanations for lower participation, citizenship education might seem more helpful. In both the American and British political systems, political parties operate an oligopoly, because the systems make effective competition from start-ups incredibly difficult. So parties target the median voter, to the enormous detriment of political debate, with the effect that reliable information is difficult to access for citizens. Most US voters are expected to participate at 10 or more levels of government, and US political parties are notoriously loose: knowing that a candidate is a Democrat or a Republican gains one very little information about how he will behave in office. Many political issues are highly complex, and it is difficult for citizens to get, and to think about, the technical information required. Even journalists on 'serious' newspapers often have a tenuous grasp of the methods of the physical and social sciences, and little acquaintance with statistical analysis, so their presentation of complex issues is often simply wrong.

Even in so far as subjective factors are responsible for the decline, these might be better addressed through the reform of systems rather than of citizenship education. Imagine, for example, that Sandy is an articulate, well-informed and reasonable person, habituated to consider carefully other people's points of views and arguments, and willing to revise his own views in the light of that thought. What reason would he have had to vote in the 2004 US Presidential race? The two main candidates were not very far apart on most issues of substance. The candidates refrained from campaigning in most States, because the structure of the electoral system ensured that the election would be decided in a few battleground States. Unless Sandy inhabited a battleground State, he had every reason to believe that, even if he passionately supported one candidate, his vote was not worth registering. As for participating in the campaigns: since both candidates relied almost entirely on contributions from wealthy donors and a 'Get-out-the-vote' strategy in which volunteers never engage other people in discussions of the issues, Sandy would find little opportunity there to exercise his virtues as a citizen. He might try to participate in lower-level political races, but in that case he might find it extremely difficult to access reliable information about candidates.

The numerous levels of government, and the complexity of ballot-access laws, mean that the party systems in each are not well-aligned with those in the others. Consider the following offices: US President (4-yr term); US Senate (6-yr term); US Congress (2 yr-term); State Governor (4-yr term); State Officers such as Treasurer and Supervisor of Education (typically 4-yr); State Senate (2–4-yr), State Representative (typically 2-yr); County Judicial Posts (typically 2–4-yr); County Executive; County Supervisor; City Mayor; City Councillor; and other County and City Offices like District Attorney, Clerk, etc (all typically 2–4 yr). Almost all of these posts have primaries as well as general elections. Local races in many

States are non-partisan; that is, the ballot papers do not contain information about the party membership of the candidate, and among the other races the party affiliation of the candidates for local, State, and national offices carry very different kinds of information. Reform of the electoral, campaign finance, and deliberative systems would be much more helpful to Sandy than increased citizenship education.

Nevertheless schools have to face the fact that such reform will be slow in coming, and it may well be true that, however inefficiently, citizenship education might help to address these subjective factors. To do so it would have to focus on illuminating the structure of the political system, and convey strategies for gathering information, and for evaluating it by, for example, acquainting students with some of the basic principles of statistical analysis. It is not a panacea, but it is not necessarily useless.

The foregoing remarks, if they are right, suggest that non-school-related reforms might be more helpful to producing responsible participation by citizens. However, in the absence of those reforms schools, once again, can expect to have to take up the educational slack. The right kind of citizenship education might help us to produce better citizens. But can we expect to get the right kind of citizenship education?

Think about the problems. First, citizenship education programmes have to have the right kinds of aims; they must focus on the quite demanding conception of reasonable citizenship that I elaborated in Chapter Four. The problem is that each body proposing citizenship education has its own conception of good citizenship; and some bodies do not even disclose their conceptions. So, for example, the Indiana standards I quoted above promote 'greater voter turnout, service on juries, and involvement in community endeavors for improvement', but say nothing about being able to engage reasonably with the arguments of others, or holding back from advancing claims that one cannot justify by appeal to common reason. The *Crick Report*, which argued for introducing citizenship education in the UK, emphasizes a duty to participate in public affairs, but not to reason carefully about one's participation.[2]

Second, citizenship education requires a large pool of teachers who are well equipped to teach the relevant habits, information, and skills. Even the principles of statistical analysis are difficult to teach, and both the US and the UK face severe shortages of qualified mathematics teachers. But the teacher of citizenship education would need a good grounding not only in statistics, but also in a wide range of other subjects, such as history, political theory, and economics.

Teaching children how to reason and argue reasonably about contentious and emotionally charged issues may be even more difficult. Teachers will naturally be nervous about the sensitivities of their students, and about the forces outside the classroom that are ready to pounce if they exceed their remit. Some parents will fear that their children are being indoctrinated; others will fear that their children are not being sufficiently challenged, but are merely having the prejudices confirmed. In a heterogeneous classroom, it will be hard to avoid fuelling at least one of these fears.

Recent research into the teaching of social and ethical issues arising from developments in biomedical research found that teachers deal with such issues in very different ways.[3] To summarize: science teachers felt that it was their role to teach 'the facts' and they were insufficiently equipped to deal with the ethics involved. Humanities teachers, on the other hand, viewed the teaching of controversial issues as relatively unproblematic but often felt that the scientific facts in accessible form were not always readily available to them. The research does not, however, explore what humanities teachers think values are and whether, for example, they endorse moral relativism or objectivity about values.

My surmise from this and other research is that currently few teachers are well equipped to do the teaching about controversial issues that citizenship education would inevitably involve. Too many teachers on both sides of the science/humanities divide seem to think that there is a simple 'fact/value' distinction, and that the standards for thinking about each side of the distinction are completely different. Professionals preparing resources for citizenship education, and providing training for the teachers, will have to work hard to overcome the sense of both children and many teachers that there are no rigorous standards for thinking about values. Teacher education itself needs to take this on board. In the United States most universities have numerous faculties that have a good deal of experience in teaching controversial issues, but they are not in education schools, but in philosophy, rhetoric, and political science departments. Faculties that teach controversial issues work out fairly quickly that they need to be extremely well informed about the issues themselves, to facilitate discussion and identify when it is likely to become explosive, and to be adept at thinking through the moral questions students raise on their feet. Teacher educators would do well to tap that expertise, but also to guide it. (Philosophers, in particular, are not renowned for their sense of how things work in the world outside the academy.)

Third, both the authorities designing the curricular demands and the teachers themselves must be conscious of the possibility of political bias in their teaching, and must be well equipped to avoid bias. James Tooley, one of the few critical voices when CE was introduced in the UK, sees bias in the very design of the curriculum. He argued that the committee recommending the reform, far from employing a consensual set of values, advocated teaching a particular version of left-wing ideology:

> [I]t is pretty easy to spot a tad of political bias creeping into the [Crick] report at every stage. After all 'ethical trading, peace-making and peace-keeping', and 'poverty, famine, disease, charity and human rights', all seem to be recognizably the building blocks of a discernible political creed, one focussed on underdevelopment, the evils of global capitalism, and how the United Nations can put it all right. Meanwhile 'prejudice, xenophobia, discrimination, pluralism' and 'equal opportunities and gender equality' likewise could be the building blocks of another left-wing political creed'.[4]

Actually, there are two possible ways of taking this objection. The first is that the values are wrong and should not be taught, nor serve as the basis for the framework in which citizenship is taught. In fact I think that the charge of left-wing bias against the Crick report is harsh: though (as a left-winger myself) I find it harsher to non-left wingers than it is to the committee that produced the report. Right-wingers believe in ethical trading: they just believe in a different ethical standard than left-wingers. They, too, believe in peace-making and peace-keeping, though they dispute with left-wingers, as left-wingers dispute amongst themselves, how it is best done and what is the best agency for it. It is quite hard to find right-wingers who are opposed to charity: to be fair it has traditionally been the left that has been suspicious of charity. Xenophobia is not the exclusive property of the right (as I, a foreigner who has long lived within American left-wing circles, know only too well), and sober left-wingers are aware of how cosmopolitan many right-wingers are.

The disagreements between left and right are simply not captured by the terms Tooley cites: they are disagreements about how to interpret the pertinent values, how much weight to give them, and how to institutionalize them. One of the vital tasks of citizenship educators (and of educators in general, whether of citizenship or not) is to ensure that their students come to understand precisely this, and to develop the critical skills that enable them to reflect rationally on political debate. So while I agree with Tooley that educators should avoid political bias, I see nothing special or unusual about citizenship education in this respect. The best way to ensure this is to teach pupils themselves the important skills of detecting bias and indoctrination.

The second way of taking Tooley's comment is that even if the values were right, it would be improper for the government to use them as the basis for teaching citizenship, because they are disputed among reasonable people. Why would anyone think that the right values should not be taught to children? The view might *seem* outlandish, but it isn't. This version of Tooley's worry is closely connected, in fact, to the conception of liberal legitimacy that underlies the view of good citizenship I advanced in Chapter Four. I argued there that good citizens will refrain from demanding measures which they can justify only by appeal to reasons that they know other people could not accept, because they are, in some deep sense, private. The reason this is so important is that the legitimate state is able to command the consent of its reasonable citizens; and a state that justified its actions on the basis of reasons that they could not accept would forfeit the right to that consent.

In the formulation I've been using, I have not made it a requirement of legitimacy that citizens actually do consent to the state. That demand would be too strong: it doesn't tell against legitimacy that unreasonable, bloody-minded, or insane citizens dissent. But I have also said nothing about the mechanisms that produce consent. Recall the discussion in Chapter Six where we saw that legitimating consent must be earned, not manufactured, even if the state in question in some sense deserves the consent it gets. The problem with citizenship education is that it might support the concern that the state is gaining consent in a non-legitimate way. It might be that teaching citizenship education is relevantly like slipping a consent-inducing drug into the water supply.

There is something to this fear. But again, how much weight to give it depends on the conception of citizenship picked out, and on the way it is taught. Consider the following, and chilling, comments by William Galston, a political theorist who served as a domestic policy advisor to the White House during Bill Clinton's first term as President:

[I]t would be rash to conclude that the clash between rational inquiry and civic education in liberal societies has ceased to exist . . . On the practical level, few individuals will come to embrace the core commitments of liberal society through a process of rational inquiry. If children are to be brought up to accept these commitments as valid and binding, the method must be pedagogy that is far more rhetorical than rational. For example, rigorous historical research will almost certainly vindicate complex 'revisionist' accounts of key figures in American history. Civic education, however,

requires a nobler, moralizing history: a pantheon of heroes
who confer legitimacy on central institutions and are worthy
of emulation. It is unrealistic to believe that more than a few
adult citizens of liberal societies will ever move beyond the
kind of civic commitment engendered by such a pedagogy.[5]

I have already cast doubt on the propriety of teaching patriotic attachment, but what Galston is suggesting here is that
whatever the virtues of good citizenship, it is over-optimistic
to expect them to be developed in response to evidence and
argument. An emotional hook is needed and, in the normal
case, that hook will be constructed in a way that is misleading.
This, if you like, is what the myth of Rosa Parks as a 'tired old
black seamstress' we encountered in the previous chapter
does; it hooks the students into a certain conception of good
citizenship through a story that has more emotional power
for a child or a teenager than the true story of a calculating
and well-organized movement of troublemakers.

The moralizing pedagogy Galston recommends is not free
of practical dangers. When a government permits such a
pedagogy, it places the elite with easy access to the 'revisionist' history in the uncomfortable situation which can lead to
contempt either for the institutions of the state, or for the
mass whose loyalty is grounded in falsehoods. A society that
supports free inquiry and allows relatively easy access to its
results also makes it easy for agitators from that elite to
exacerbate the periodic crises of legitimacy to which any free
society is prone. Loyalty is more secure in a crisis when
grounded in informed rational reflection than when grounded
in a demagogic pedagogy.

More important, in principle, than the dubiousness of
Galston's political calculation is the relationship of his

pedagogy to the prospects for achieving actual legitimacy. Not only do Galston's civic educators aim to inculcate an unacceptably deferential citizenship, but their method involves systematically misleading future citizens, erecting serious barriers to the critical and informed consent to which legitimacy aspires.

But this does not mean that all citizenship education will be illegitimate. Instead, it suggests some guidelines for teaching citizenship education. While we are aiming to produce good citizenship, we are also aiming to do so legitimately. That means citizenship educators are required to instil, at the appropriate age, habits of sceptical enquiry into their students; inclinations to subject all values and principles, including those on which the state is founded, to rational scrutiny. They should avoid deploying misleading myths in the service of citizenship education. Moreover, while they are entitled, especially when teaching younger children, to use emotional hooks to engage their students in learning, they need to scrutinize these hooks for bias and for their tendency to inhibit reflective reason.

Now to a final worry about teaching citizenship education. The conception of citizenship I have advanced can probably be inculcated only if we encourage students to rationally scrutinize their own political commitments and presuppositions, and those of others. But, as Amy Gutmann, who developed the conception of citizenship I am supporting, has pointed out, the skills involved in 'political reflection cannot be neatly differentiated from the skills involved in evaluating one's own way of life'.[6]

Most (if not all) of the same skills and virtues that are necessary and sufficient for educating children for citizenship

in a liberal democracy are those that are necessary and
sufficient for educating children to deliberate about their own
ways of life, more generally (and less politically) speaking.[7]

The advocate of citizenship education of the form I am supporting faces the same problem that the advocate of autonomy-
facilitating education will face: that some parents will strongly
resist an educational regime in which their children are, however indirectly, encouraged and equipped to reflect rationally
and critically on the received views of their parents.

One response to this worry is simply to stand firm. Because
those parents have no right to impose their own views in their
children, schools do nothing wrong by encouraging critical
reflection. But this general stance might have very serious
costs in term of the very value that we are trying to promote –
viz., good citizenship. Consider, again, the Mozert case discussed in Chapter Five. The Mozert parents objected to their
children being subject to a very mild form of citizenship
education on precisely the grounds that it would undermine
their belief in the parents' religious views. The state, in effect,
stood firm against them. The children themselves ended up in
fundamentalist religious schools, the non-religious children
within the public schools were deprived of the heterogeneity
their presence created, and sectarian religious entrepreneurs
had another powerful story with which to foster alienation
between fundamentalist Christians and mainstream public
institutions. It is hard for me to believe that, in that particular
case, the consequences of standing firm for fostering good
citizenship were superior to the consequences of a more
deferential stance. In the United States it is especially difficult
for the 'stand firm' strategy to have good overall consequences because recalcitrant parents always have resort to

withdrawing their children into virtually unregulated private schools.

For this reason it seems to me that the right strategy will vary according to context. Policymakers should be as deferential to parents as necessary to produce the best outcomes in the context, and deferential in the ways that will produce the best outcomes. In the UK I suspect officials can afford to be less deferential than in the US, where there is much more popular opposition to particular elements of citizenship education, and where the public culture is more likely to be affected by disputes in ways that are detrimental to the production of good citizenship.

In conclusion, the case for making citizenship education compulsory is much more complicated than it might have appeared when I argued for the goal of producing good citizens in Chapter Four. The problems with teaching citizenship do not weigh decisively against it. However, they do help both to caution us to the need for resources and education for teachers who are charged with teaching citizenship, and also to be conscious of some of the dangers of teaching citizenship the wrong way.

The guiding normative idea of this book has been that education should promote human flourishing, when human flourishing is understood in a pluralistic fashion. In Part One I explained that this means four central ideals that should inform the curriculum and ethos of schooling. First I argued that schooling should facilitate the powerful interest children have in becoming autonomous, self-governing adults. Second I argued that it should enable them to become economically self-reliant, in so far as that is possible, and that this and the other goals should take precedence over the growth demands of the economy. Third, I argued that it should enhance children's prospective wellbeing more generally considered. Finally I argued that schooling should aim to produce responsible, deliberative citizens who are capable of accepting the demands of justice and abiding by the norm of reciprocity.

In Part Two I looked at three controversial issues concerning schooling today. I argued that state support for religious schools is quite compatible with the values advocated in the first section, and, in some circumstances at least, is the best course of action. I showed that inculcating patriotism through schooling was extremely problematic; and finally I argued that, although citizenship education is entirely appropriate, it is unlikely to be a panacea, and also very difficult to implement well.

Guiding my discussion of all the institutional issues is the idea that the goals I have set in Part One are not in fact goals of schooling, but of education, a process that involves parents, schools, and other public institutions, including the culture more generally. So what schools should actually do, and how they should be structured, depends on how best to achieve the goals in the actual social context they inhabit, taking into account the feedback effects the structure of schooling has on the rest of the institutions including the family.

It might seem a bit of a cheat to mention this only in the conclusion, but I have neglected several complexities, which I would like to highlight here.

The first is that I have not talked at all about the distribution of educational opportunities; and the possibility that a fair distribution might interfere with some of the goals I've mentioned. If, for example, a fair distribution required that everyone be educated so that they encountered each other as equals in the labour market, that might conflict with the goal of facilitating children's long-term wellbeing. Consider the cultural dislocation experienced by children from immigrant backgrounds if they decide to pursue careers that require them to assimilate into the mainstream culture. For some children, facilitating these careers may have the long-term effect of undermining some important sources of flourishing for them. This is, I think, quite a serious problem for educators of some working-class and immigrant children, and I have been quiet about it partly because I do not think I have anything very enlightening to say about it.

Similarly, I have made the simplifying assumption throughout that the goals argued for in Part One are congruent; that is, that they can be pursued simultaneously and effectively. I believe that in ideal circumstances that is true, but, as I have acknowledged, we do not operate in ideal circumstances. There might be conflicts between promoting good citizenship, or facilitating autonomy, and promoting flourishing in the way I've understood it. I have neglected this possibility not because I have nothing to say but because I wanted, in a short book, to display the structure of how to think about the relationships between particular values and the institution of schooling. Matters are much more complicated when we consider the possibility of incongruence between the values and what that might demand of us as educators and policymakers. I hope that the case I have made here at least provides readers with a framework for thinking about the conflicts.

I have also completely neglected the possible conflict between pursuing these goals and what I think of as a constraint on compulsory education. Schooling is a future-directed activity; we are fostering the development of knowledge, skills, and habits in the children we teach that will serve them well when they become adults. But it happens in the present: children are forced to attend schools for some 15–20,000 hours of their lives between the ages of 4 and 18. Even if they were not forced, they would be under enormous pressure to attend, because so much of their future wellbeing depends on being schooled. If the place a child is forced to attend makes her life miserable for that time, she is subject to a serious harm. Schools must be places in which the immediate wellbeing of every individual child is taken seriously and fostered. The harms schooling can impose are various: a child can be put in serious physical danger, or can be psychologically bullied, or can be simply made lonely. School administrators are obliged to structure their schools so that they are pleasant places for children to be, and need to ensure that no child is being subject to conditions that make her schooldays unhappy.

I should emphasize that I am not suggesting that teachers should be constantly attentive to children's self-esteem, still less that they should 'dumb down' the curriculum for the sake of fostering self-esteem. Self-esteem is often better served by a challenging academic curriculum rigorously presented than by attempting to foster self-esteem directly. It is also hard for schools to know how to foster self-esteem without more information about the child's home life than is usually available. But the will and the systems needed to prevent schooldays being miserable might sometimes take resources away from some of the other goals schools ought to be pursuing. I have ignored the possibility of this conflict, and I wouldn't want to say that when it happens the goal of avoiding misery is always more important. But it is an important goal, and one that should not be entirely neglected in the pursuit of future-oriented goals.

I would like, finally, to reiterate a comment I made in the introduction. Society places enormous demands on schools and teachers, and gives them remarkably little support. Politicians are constantly asking for higher achievement scores and blaming teachers when they are not forthcoming; and, sometimes, blaming testing services for lax standards when these scores are forthcoming. In the US and the UK macroeconomic policy maintains high levels of child poverty, but policymakers expect schools to do as well as schools in societies which have all but eliminated child poverty. Many children are imbued in a materialist public culture that disvalues learning and intellectual life, and celebrates money and unearned fame. They spend thousands of hours in the course of their childhoods watching advertisements for things that are bad for them, made by people who have no interest at all in the wellbeing of the children they are advertising to. Parents are much less inclined to trust schools, and to back them up when they make demands of children or try to impose discipline, than they were 40 years ago. Real spending on schooling has increased over that time, but not in line with the increased expectations that schools teach children with special educational needs and from high-need backgrounds. Simultaneously, the hidden subsidy that public schooling enjoyed from the fact that talented women were formally or informally excluded from other professions has evaporated. Schools are, in other words, given a task which is difficult in the best of circumstances, but are told to do it in circumstances which are not the best. They are then blamed for not living up to impossibly high standards.

I suppose the readers of this book fall into two categories – teachers and non-teachers. I hope that teachers will not have found my arguments censorious, but will take them seriously and subject them to critique in the light of their own experiences and reason. I hope that non-teachers will do the same, but also, if they are persuaded by my arguments, that they will see themselves, and society as a whole, as responsible for creating an out-of-school environment for children that supports, rather than inhibits, schools in their pursuit of these goals.

Notes

INTRODUCTION

1 Interested readers might want to look at Harry Brighouse, *School Choice and Social Justice* (Oxford: Oxford University Press, 2000) and UK readers might look at Harry Brighouse, *A Level Playing Field: Reforming Private Schools* (London: Fabian Society, 2000).

CHAPTER ONE EDUCATING FOR SELF-GOVERNMENT

1 Joseph Raz, *The Morality of Freedom* (Oxford: Oxford University Press, 1987), pp. 369–70.

2 See Juliet Schor, *Born to Buy* (New York: Scribner, 2004) and Susan Linn, *Consuming Kids* (New York: Basic Books, 2004) for detailed accounts of the way that marketers attempt to undermine personal autonomy.

3 See Gerald M. Nosich, *Learning to Think Things Through: A Guide to Critical Thinking in the Curriculum* (Upper Saddle River, NJ: Prentice Hall, 2001) who makes much stronger arguments to the effect that the curriculum provides us with frameworks for understanding and analysing the world (much more than 'information' or 'facts'), which enable us to think critically about a variety of matters.

4 J.S. Mill, *On Liberty* (New York: Norton, 1975), p. 36.

CHAPTER TWO EDUCATING FOR ECONOMIC PARTICIPATION

1 Labour Party, *The Skills Revolution* (1996), quoted in Alison Wolf, *Does Education Matter?* (London: Penguin, 2002), p 13.

2 For interesting discussions of the role of work in a flourishing life, see

Howard Gardner, Mihaly Csikszentmhalyi and William Damon, *Good Work* (New York: Basic Books, 2001), Tim Kasser, *The High Price of Materialism* (Cambridge Mass.: MIT Press, 2002), and Richard Layard, *Happiness* (London: Penguin, 2005).

3 World Bank, *Priorities and Strategies for Education. A World Bank Review* (1995).

4 Robert Frank, *Luxury Fever* (Princeton, Ill: Princeton University Press, 1999), p. 72.

5 Ibid., p. 73.

6 Ibid., p. 72.

7 Fred Hirsch, *Social Limits to Growth* (Cambridge, Mass.: Harvard University Press, 1976). For a wonderfully accessible account of the contemporary economies influenced by Hirsch's ideas, see Robert Frank and Phillip Cook, *The Winner Take All Society* (London: Penguin, 1996).

CHAPTER THREE   EDUCATING FOR FLOURISHING

1 Richard Layard, *Happiness* (London: Penguin, 2005) pp. 62–70.

2 This is obvious to songwriters and comedians, even if philosophers have a hard time with it. As Ken Dodd says, 'When you go to measuring a man's success, don't count money, count happiness'.

3 See Linda Waite, *The Case for Marriage* (New York: Doubleday, 2000).

4 Juliet Schor, *Born to Buy* (New York: Scribner, 2004), p. 21.

5 Ibid., p. 57.

6 See Tim Kasser, *The High Price of Materialism* (Cambridge, Mass.: MIT Press, 2002) for summaries of the evidence.

7 Orlando Patterson, *Freedom in the Modern World* (New York: Basic Books, forthcoming).

8 Kasser, pp. 82, 85–6.

9 Schor, chapter 8.

10 G. Whitty, G. Rowe and P. Aggleton, 'Subjects and Themes in the Secondary School Curriculum', *Research Papers In Education*, vol. 9, no. 2, 1994.

11 'Try It and See', *The Economist*, 28 February 2002.

12 If, that is, the experiences are not poisoned by response to the perverse incentives built into the college admissions process, as in the United States, where colleges put considerable weight on demonstrating that one is a high-level participant in extra-curricular activities.

CHAPTER FOUR   CREATING CITIZENS

1 See Adam Swift, *How Not to Be A Hypocrite: School Choice for the Morally Perplexed* (London: RoutledgeFalmer, 2003) for a fascinating discussion of the moral principles at stake in choosing schools for one's children.

2 Amy Gutmann and Dennis Thompson, *Democracy and Deliberation* (Cambridge, Mass.: Harvard University Press, 1994), p. 57.

CHAPTER FIVE   SHOULD GOVERNMENTS SUPPORT RELIGIOUS SCHOOLS?

1 Anthony Grayling, 'Keep God out of Public Affairs', *Observer*, 12 August, 2001.

2 Sandra Feldman, 'A Commentary on Public Education and Other Critical Issues', *The New York Times*, 3 October, 1999 (advertisement).

3 I claim no expertise in constitutional scholarship. But it seems reasonable to expect rigorous moral reasoning to inform constitutional interpretation.

4 For a full account of the case, see Stephen Bates, *Battleground: One Mother's Crusade, the Religious Right, and the Struggle for Control of Our Classrooms* (New York: Poseidon Press/Simon & Schuster, 1993).

5 In fact, the average size of a US high school is about 650 students, but most students attend much larger schools.

6 I don't mean to let them off the hook; they are, indeed, committing a serious error. However, I doubt that most of them are committing the wrong that religious believers might be justified, but mistaken, in attributing to them. I've explained why, precisely, they are wrong in 'Channel One, the Anti-Commercial Principle, and the Discontinuous Ethos', *Educational Policy*, vol. 19, no. 3, 2005.

CHAPTER SIX   SHOULD SCHOOLS TEACH PATRIOTISM?

1 Lynne Cheney, 'The End of History', *Wall Street Journal*, 20 October 1994, p. A 22.

2 Ibid.

3 Gary Nash, Charlotte Crabtree, and Ross E. Dunn, *History on Trial*, (New York: Vintage Books, 2000), p. 15.

4 Daniel J. Boorstin, *A History of the United States since 1861* (Needhan, Mass.: Pearson/Prentice Hall, 2005).

5 Nick Tate, 'They Come Not to Praise England but to Bury It', *The Sunday Times*, 27 August 2000.

6 Ibid.

7 Quoted in 'Make History Compulsory – Tories' at http://news.bbc.co.uk/1/hi/education/4209075.stm, accessed 18 April 2005 at 10.00 am CST.

8 Taken from David Miller, 'In Defence of Nationality', *Journal of Applied Philosophy*, vol. 10, no. 1 (1993): 3–16.

9 Leon Rosselson, *For the Good of the Nation* (London: Journeyman Press, 1981), p. 13.

10 I have no serious data on what people actually believe about Rosa Parks, but everyone I have tested with this question who was not, already, a committed left-winger of some sort, was quite unaware of her role as a political organizer.

CHAPTER SEVEN   SHOULD CITIZENSHIP EDUCATION BE COMPULSORY?

1 'About Citizenship Education', *Indiana Department of Public Instruction*, at http://www.doe.state.in.us/charactered/citizenshiped.html (accessed 18 April 2005 at 10.30 am CST).

2 *Education for Citizenship and the Teaching of Democracy in Schools*, (London: Qualifications and Curriculum Authority, 1998).

3 R. Levinson *et al.*, 'Constraints on Teaching the Social and Ethical Issues Arising from Developments in Biomedical Research: A View across the Curriculum in England and Wales', in R. Cross and P. Fensham (eds), *Science and the Citizen. For Educators and the Public*. A special issue of Melbourne Studies In Education. (Melbourne: Arena Publications, 2000).

4 James Tooley, *Reclaiming Education* (London and New York: Cassell 2000), p. 145.

5 William Galston, *Liberal Purposes* (New York and Cambridge: Cambridge University Press 1991).

6 A. Gutmann, 'Civic Education and Social Diversity', *Ethics*, vol. 105, no. 3, (1995), p. 578.

7 Ibid., p. 573.

Related titles from Routledge

On the Internet
Hubert L. Dreyfus

'A well-crafted polemic ... we need more teachers like Dreyfus himself, integrating the web into courses that are still deeply human.' **Adam Morton, Times Literary Supplement**

'interesting and definitely much needed ... a short and thought provoking book that can be read by any net enthusiast and/or scholar who is interested in the topics of learning, knowledge and identity in relation to the Internet' **Humanist**

Drawing on a diverse array of thinkers from Plato to Kierkegaard, *On the Internet* is one of the first books to bring philosophical insight to the debate on how far the internet can and cannot take us.

Dreyfus shows us the roots of the disembodied, free floating web surfer in Descartes' separation of mind and body, and how Kierkegaard's insights into the birth of the modern reading public anticipate the news-hungry, but disinterested risk avoiding internet junkie. Drawing on recent studies of the isolation experienced by many internet users, Dreyfus shows how the internet's privatisation of experience ignores essential human capacities such as trust, moods, risk, shared local concerns and commitment. *On the Internet* is essential reading for anyone on line and all those interested in our place in the e-revolution.

Hb: 0-415-22806-9
Pb: 0-415-22807-7

Available at all good bookshops
For ordering and further information please visit:
www.routledge.com

Related titles from Routledge

On Religion
John D. Caputo

'Intellectual without being overly academic ... one cheers his vigour and relishes his insights into the paradoxical, ambiguous nature of religion and religious belief. Recommended.' **Library Journal (US)**

'With some deft sophistry (heavily influenced by Derrida who also produced one of the other five books in the Routledge's new Thinking in Action series) John D Caputo redefines religion as love of the unforeseeable. And, as that is a given in life, his definition of religiosity pretty much equates with my definition of joie de vivre. So the opposite of a religious person is not an atheist, merely a "pusillanimous curmudgeon". But it's not all just clever wordplay. With his unorthodox definitions in place, Caputo goes on to denounce dogma, put Marx, Nietzsche and Freud in their historical places and to reunite religion, mysticism and science. On top of all that, there's a detailed deconstruction of religion in Star Wars. I'm converted.' **Laurence Phelan, The Independent on Sunday**

'I feel obliged to warn readers that I loved this book. I loved its passion, loved its ideas, and the loved the alternately sassy and incantatory rhythms of its prose ... get this book and read it' **Sea of Faith**

On Religion is a thrilling and accessible exploration of religious faith today. If God is dead, why is religion back? Digging up the roots of all things religious, John D. Caputo inspects them with clarity and style. Along the way, some fascinating questions crop up: What do I love when I love my God? What can the film Star Wars tell us about religion and what does "may the force be with you" really mean? What are people doing when they perform an act "in the name of God" ?

Hb: 0-415-23332-1
Pb: 0-415-23333-x

Available at all good bookshops
For ordering and further information please visit:
www.routledge.com

Related titles from Routledge

On Humanism
Richard Norman

'This outline of the humanist philosophy of life by Richard Norman is first class. It covers the history, philosophy, morality and meaning of humanism with extreme clarity ... a book of great lucidity, considerable thought and grace.' **New Humanist**

'A lucid account of humanism which combines the virtues of a fairly balanced discussion and a passionate polemic. It deserves to become humanism's unofficial manifesto - the only kind a freethinking movement can have.' **Julian Baggini, author of Atheism: A Very Short Introduction**

humanism /'hju:meniz(e)m/ n. an outlook or system of thought concerned with human rather than divine or supernatural matters.

Albert Einstein, Isaac Asimov, E.M. Forster, Bertrand Russell, and Gloria Steinem all declared themselves humanists. What is humanism and why does it matter? Is there any doctrine every humanist must hold? If it rejects religion, what does it offer in its place? Have the twentieth century's crimes against humanity spelled the end for humanism?

On Humanism is a timely and powerfully argued philosophical defence of humanism. It is also an impassioned plea that we turn to ourselves, not religion, if we want to answer Socrates' age-old question: what is the best kind of life to lead? Although humanism has much in common with science, Richard Norman shows that it is far from a denial of the more mysterious, fragile side of being human. He deals with big questions such as the environment, Darwinism and 'creation science', euthanasia and abortion, and then argues that it is ultimately through the human capacity for art, literature and the imagination that humanism is a powerful alternative to religious belief.

Drawing on a varied range of examples from Aristotle to Primo Levi and the novels of Virginia Woolf and Graham Swift, *On Humanism* is a lucid and much needed reflection on this much talked about but little understood phenomenon.

Hb: 0-415-30522-5
Pb: 0-415-30523-3

Available at all good bookshops
For ordering and further information please visit:

www.routledge.com

Related titles from Routledge

On Evil

Adam Morton

'This essay elucidates a picture of those who commit "evil" acts as lacking a mental "barrier" to stop them, using examples from recent history and pop-culture treatments from Buffy to Hannibal Lecter ... ' **Steven Poole, The Guardian**

'The author actually does what too few academics do: exhibit thought in action, not substituting the stale cite for an original idea.' **Fred Alford, author of What Evil Means to Us**

Evil has long fascinated psychologists, philosophers, novelists and playwrights but remains an incredibly difficult concept to talk about.

On Evil is a compelling and at times disturbing tour of the many faces of evil. What is evil, and what makes people do awful things? If we can explain evil, do we explain it away? Can we imagine the mind of a serial killer, or does such evil defy description? Does evil depend on a contrast with good, as religion tells us, or can there be evil for evil's sake?

Adam Morton argues that any account of evil must help us understand three things: why evil occurs; why evil often arises out of banal or everyday situations; and how we can be seen as evil. Drawing on fascinating examples as diverse as Augustine, Buffy the Vampire Slayer, psychological studies of deviant behaviour and profiles of serial killers, Adam Morton argues that evil occurs when internal, mental barriers against it simply break down. Adam Morton also introduces us to some nightmare people, such as Adolf Eichmann and Hannibal Lecter, reminding us that understanding their actions as humans brings us closer to understanding evil.

Exciting and thought-provoking, *On Evil* is essential reading for anyone interested in a topic that attracts and repels us in equal measure.

Hb: 0-415-30518-7
Pb: 0-415-30519-5

Available at all good bookshops
For ordering and further information please visit:
www.routledge.com